READING INTO
SCIENCE
PHYSICS

Averil Macdonald

Published in 2003 by:
Nelson Thornes Ltd
Delta Place
27 Bath Road
CHELTENHAM
GL53 7TH
United Kingdom

03 04 05 06 / 10 9 8 7 6 5 4 3 2 1

A catalogue record for this book is available from the British Library

ISBN 0 7487 6801 7

Illustrations by Ian Foulis, Francis Bacon and Mike Bastin
Design and page make-up by Jordan Publishing Design

Printed and bound in Spain by Graficas

INTRODUCTION

The *Reading Into Science* series is for the Ideas and Evidence part of your GCSE. It covers a whole range of topics from historical figures to interviews with some real scientists I know who are making new discoveries now. I have included some articles about when scientists got things wrong in the past – and even how they may be getting things wrong today! On top of that I've tackled some very controversial topics like are mobile phones dangerous and is nuclear power really all bad? These articles will give you the bottom line – exactly what you need to make up your own mind!

Some articles are harder to read than others. Blue arrows alongside the page numbers, show the more complicated ones. Red arrows show which ones are more straightforward.

There are questions at the end of each article. Use these to practise answering the sort of questions you will get in your final exam.

Finally there are web site addresses in case you want to follow up any of the ideas – or you can check out the *Reading Into Science* web site on **www.nelsonthornes.com/ris**.

I hope you find these articles interesting. I certainly enjoyed researching and writing them. Let me know what you thought through the Nelson Thornes website.

Averil Macdonald

CONTENTS

If there were a prize for the most important invention of the 20th century it should go to the transistor. This tiny device started life as a way to solve the problem that telephone calls could not be transmitted across country without fading away. By the end of the century it had spawned the Internet.

« Bill Shockley, John Bardeen and Walter Brattain were great friends – until success came between them »

Bill Shockley, John Bardeen and Walter Brattain first became friends when they were working at Bell Laboratories, an important research company in the USA. They were given the job of using the newly developed semiconductor materials to build a switch that could boost or amplify electronic telephone signals. There was a device that could do it already, the triode valve, but it was too expensive and tended to get too hot. They needed something better.

Shockley's first attempt didn't work and he gave Bardeen and Brattain the job of finding out why. It seemed that condensation kept forming on the device, stopping it working. They thought about putting it into a vacuum jar to get rid of the condensation but couldn't be bothered. (If there's no air then there can be no water to condense on the device.) To save time Brattain decided to dunk the whole thing underwater to remove the condensation. It worked! Only a little bit, but it worked!

They kept on experimenting with different ideas but it was only when Bardeen had a brain wave that it

Semiconductors are halfway between conductors and insulators – but cleverer than that. Conductors are materials that allow an electric current to flow easily. Wires in electric circuits are made of metals because metals are good conductors. At the other end of the range are electrical insulators. These are materials, like plastics, which do not allow an electric current to flow through them. Wires are encased in plastic because the plastic insulator does not allow the electric current to escape from the wire if someone touches it. Between conductors and insulators are semiconductors. Natural semiconductors are materials like silicon and germanium. They conduct only a little under normal circumstances. The reason they are so useful is that small amounts of other materials like arsenic or boron can be added to the semiconductor and this makes it conduct a lot more. In this way we can control exactly how much a semiconductor conducts electricity – a real designer material.

BC 108

« This little device doesn't look like much but it changed the future of information and communications technology »

Electric current can flow through good conductors because these materials have 'free electrons'. These electrons do not orbit their parent atoms like most electrons. Instead they flow freely past the atoms of the material. When a voltage is applied all these free electrons start to drift towards the positive terminal. This is an electric current. Bardeen used his imagination to work out that although electrons can flow freely through the solid itself, they do not flow freely at the surface. Instead they form a barrier which stops other charge flowing. It is when a scientist has the nerve to break away from standard ideas and use his or her imagination like this that they make a breakthrough.

finally solved the problem. He decided immediately that he had to go one better and spent the next four weeks working out how to build an even better device.

Now it was Brattain and Bardeen's turn to feel angry that they had been left out. There were arguments about who should have their name on the patent and get all the publicity. From then on the team fell apart.

The media were unimpressed when the invention of the transistor was announced

The tiny device was announced to the world in 1948. It was named the 'transistor' from 'transfer-resistor'. By controlling the current onto the base of the transistor you can alter the current that it allows to flow through another main circuit. It seems, therefore, to

The resistance of a circuit is a measure of how easily the current can flow. If you double the resistance in a circuit and then apply the same voltage, you will find the current halves as it finds it twice as hard to flow. Ohm's law puts this into an equation:

$$V = I \times R$$

all started to come together. He realised that all the other scientists were wrong when they said that electrons drifted past atoms in a solid. In fact when the electrons are at the surface they form a barrier which stops the charge flowing. Once they understood this, Brattain and Bardeen kept on working, but without telling Shockley what they were doing.

Shockley was furious when they called him to tell him they had

transfer a resistance to the main circuit.

The media were unimpressed when the invention of the transistor was announced and most electronics companies couldn't think of any uses for it. Then two Japanese scientists had the idea of mass-producing tiny radios using transistors instead of old-fashioned valves. They founded Sony Electronics and the rest is history.

« With thousands of devices on a single silicon chip, devices can be smaller and faster than anyone ever thought possible. Without these there would be no world wide web »

By 1956, the world had begun to realise how important the transistor was and the three scientists were awarded the Nobel Prize for their invention. But even then they could have had no real idea how much they had changed the world.

Now Information Technology (IT) has an enormous influence on the world. The integrated circuits (called silicon chips) in computers have thousands of separate devices (including transistors) built onto the same piece of silicon. This means that signals are processed faster, while optical fibres less than 0.12 mm thick can carry 12 000 channels of communication as pulses of light. The final piece in the IT jigsaw is lasers of completely pure colours for everything from read-write CDs, and DVDs to 'fly-by-light' aircraft controls. ■

Questions

1   Explain briefly the difference between conductors and insulators. Give some examples of each.

2   Name some typical semiconductors. How is a semiconductor different from a conductor of electricity?

3   A transistor's name comes from the idea of 'transferring-resistance'. Explain what resistance is in an electrical circuit. What equation is usually used to work out the resistance of a circuit?

4   The article claims that the transistor is the most important invention of the 20th century. How would life be different today if the transistor had not been invented?

5   The three men started working well together but later on they worked in secret. It is important for scientists to share their ideas and publish their findings in national journals for others to read. Why is this the case?

Extra activities

1   Find out what the electrical symbol is for a transistor and what the names are for the three terminals on the transistor.

2   Find out more about what the transistor can be used for in electric circuits.

3   The pet name for another semiconducting material is gallyallyarsenide. Find out what its real name is and its chemical symbol.

WEBSITES

http://www.nobel.se

How cool can you get?

The coldest place on the planet, if not in the universe, may be Lancaster in the UK. The Physics Department holds the freezer to beat all freezers. No one can get down to absolute zero (also called 0 kelvin) but the scientists at Lancaster can get down to 7 microkelvin (0.000 007K).

At these super-cold temperatures the world is very different. Metals have no electrical resistance so Ohm's law doesn't work. This means that once you have connected a power supply to your circuit to create a current, the current will keep on flowing forever, even when the power supply is removed. In fact there is a ring of superconducting metal in the USA where the current has been going round, unaided, for over 40 years!

Some liquids are even weirder at low temperatures. Most liquids become solid at some temperature. They change state from liquid to solid as their

« The University of Lancaster Physics Department may be the coldest place in the universe »

Ohm's law states that the current in certain conductors (called ohmic conductors) varies with the voltage, assuming their temperature doesn't change. An equation to summarise this is $V = I \times R$. The R stands for resistance and shows how easily the electric current can flow through a resistor. The resistance of metals goes down as they get colder. But at about 4K (−269°C) all metals get down to zero electrical resistance. This is called 'superconducting'. Some materials lose their resistance at higher temperatures than this. They are called 'high-temperature superconductors'.

LORD KELVIN 1824–1907

Lord Kelvin was born William Thomson in Belfast in 1824. He was a child prodigy and started university at the age of eleven and became a professor at the age of 23. He was fascinated by the topic of heat. Until that time scientists had believed that heat was a type of fluid called caloric. James Prescott Joule was the first person to question this theory. Joule showed that heat was a form of energy. He and Kelvin were great friends and often worked together. Kelvin wanted to know what the lowest possible temperature was.

« Lord Kelvin predicted the lowest ever temperature – but never lived to see it »

He called it 'heat death'. He predicted it would be –273°C and suggested that a scale of temperature should begin at this temperature. He never knew that this scale of temperature would be named after him.

Kelvin also made mistakes. He calculated that if the Earth had broken off from the Sun it would have taken 100 million years to cool to its present temperature so must be 100 million years old. Biologists could not see how humans could have evolved in such a short time while geologists thought the Earth must be nearer 30 billion years old to account for rock formation. Kelvin's mistake was to miss the fact that the Earth has its own heat source – radioactive rocks – that keep it warmer than it would otherwise be. We now believe the Earth is 4500 million years old (4.5 billion years).

The kelvin scale of temperature starts at 'absolute zero' – the lowest temperature scientists believe to be possible. Absolute zero (nought kelvin or 0K) is –273°C (minus 273 degrees celsius). This means that to work out a temperature on the kelvin scale you simply add 273 to the celsius temperature. No one has ever got to a temperature of 0K. Because scientists believe it is the lowest temperature possible, there is great rivalry to see who can get nearest to this temperature.

molecules slow down and no longer move past each other. Instead the molecules take up positions next to each other and simply carry on vibrating. The cooler you go, the less they vibrate. Liquid helium refuses to solidify however cold you go. The attractive forces between its molecules are so weak they can never sit quietly alongside each other – unless you increase the pressure on them to about 30 times atmospheric pressure (3 MPa), which does stop them moving about.

More peculiar is the fact that liquid helium refuses to remain in its container at temperatures below 2.176K. Instead it can flow up the sides of the container, over the rim and down the other side. It can even escape through minute holes just a few atoms wide. The reason it can do this is because it loses its viscosity completely and so it has no resistance to flowing. It's called a superfluid.

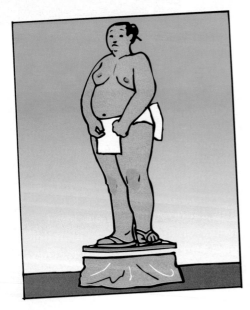

« A sumo wrestler can stand on a levitating magnet platform floating above a high-temperature superconductor. The superconductors refuse to let magnetic fields penetrate them so they keep magnets away. This is how levitating trains will work »

the star were thrown violently into space. The inner core collapsed and formed a really dense neutron star. Physicists think that neutron stars resemble raw eggs. They have a thin, hard shell on the outside and some peculiar liquids on the inside. Physicists think the liquid on the inside becomes superfluid when it cools to below 10^{11}K (100 000 000 000K) – which happens soon after the neutron star forms.

« Superfluid helium cannot be kept in a container – it will flow up the sides and escape! »

Surprisingly, hydrogen isn't a superfluid. It becomes solid at about 14K. Scientists have been looking for other superfluids for many years. Recently in Gottingen scientists have tried a number of ideas to cool hydrogen to superfluid temperatures without letting it solidify first. So far they have only managed to get this to work with 15 hydrogen molecules, so there's no guarantee that it will work with a larger sample. It's an interesting challenge.

Scientists are fascinated by superfluids, not only because atoms behave completely differently in a superfluid compared with anywhere else but also because they can tell us about what the inside of a neutron star is like.

Neutron stars seem to be superfluid. The Crab Nebula is a cloud of dust and gases that resulted from a star that exploded – a supernova. The outer layers of

Supernovae

« Supernovae are exploding stars – a rare but fascinating event in the universe »

All stars form when a nebula (a cloud of gas and dust usually left over when an old star has exploded) starts to contract because of the force of gravity between its particles. As the nebula contracts it gets hotter and hotter until nuclear reactions start and hydrogen fuses into helium. For most stars, when they have used up all their hydrogen they will start using helium and begin making heavier elements by nuclear fusion. They expand all the time and end up as red giants. Eventually when all its fuel is used up, the star will cool and contract into a white dwarf, and then keep on cooling until it is a black dwarf.

A supernova is the complete explosion of a star. The internal heat of a star makes all the particles move so fast that they exert enormous pressure. If this pressure suddenly increases the star expands – catastrophically! For example, a star the size of our Sun could expand to the size of the whole solar system in just one (Earth) day! When its fuel runs out, its centre will contract violently into a neutron star made of really dense material. A neutron star may have a mass the same as the mass of our Sun but be only 10 km across! The outer layers are thrown out into space as a nebula.

Cold and cancers

This all sounds fascinating, but is it any use? Scientists are now working on ways of using freezing (cryosurgery) to treat cancers. For external tumours, the surgeon will apply liquid nitrogen at –196°C (or 77K) directly to the tumour with a swab or a spray. This freezes the cells and kills them without having to resort to the scalpel. Normally the tumour is frozen, allowed to thaw and then frozen again to be sure the treatment is effective.

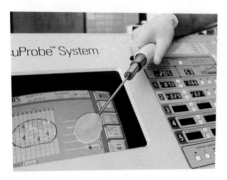

« Cryosurgery uses extremely cold temperatures to freeze tumours and treat cancers »

Recently surgeons have begun using cryosurgery for internal tumours. The liquid nitrogen is sent into a cryoprobe that is inserted through a tiny slit in the body and placed on the tumour. The surgeon uses ultrasound to create images on a screen so that he or she can monitor the treatment and make sure healthy tissue is not affected by the freezing. The advantage of cryosurgery is that there is less pain and bleeding so the patient needs a shorter stay in hospital.

Cryosurgery has been used successfully for treating skin cancer as well as prostate cancer, cervical cancer, liver cancer and a childhood cancer that affects the retina of the eye (called retinoblastoma). Now scientists are studying whether it can be used for treating bone, brain and spinal tumours.

Animals in the cold

If freezing can kill cells, it's surprising that animals can survive the intense cold of the polar regions. In fact some animals have their own built-in anti-freeze. Antarctic springtails, mites and fly larvae produce antifreeze compounds like glycerol that don't freeze even at temperatures of –40°C. Even more amazing is the wood frog that lives in Alaska. It spends most of the year with two-thirds of the water in its body frozen solid. It's not the cells in its body that freeze – that would kill it as the water froze and expanded and burst the cells like a frozen pipe bursting. Instead ice forms in the spaces between the cells. The ice then acts as an insulator and stops the water in the frog's cells from freezing. This is how the frog hibernates. There are no body functions – not even a heart beat or breathing. Then as the temperature rises in spring the frog comes back to life.

« The arctic wood frog has its own way of coping with the cold. It spends most of the year with two-thirds of the water in its body frozen »

Even the penguins suffered when the lowest temperature ever was recorded...

Even bigger animals have adapted to arctic conditions by the application of physics. The elk doesn't need thick fur on its legs to keep it warm. Instead the heat in the blood is removed before the blood flows down to its feet and is returned to the blood as the blood flows back to its body. This way the animal doesn't lose valuable body heat – and doesn't notice that its feet are cold!

Insulation

But the animals that survive the coldest climate are Antarctic penguins. Their thick layers of blubber, down and feathers insulate them against the cold, but they still need a little help from their friends if they are to survive. They all huddle together but keep shuffling round so that they take it in turns to be on the outside where the air temperature is –60°C and in the middle where the temperature is about 20°C higher.

Even the penguins suffered when the lowest temperature ever was recorded at Vostok Ice Station in Antarctica on 21 July 1989. It was –89.2°C! At this temperature boiling water poured from a kettle freezes before it hits the ground! ∎

Insulation

Good insulators almost always have trapped pockets of air in them. This is why the down and feathers of the penguin help to keep it warm. The pockets of air trapped between its feathers prevent its body heat from being conducted away.

« The penguins are well insulated but still need to huddle together to generate enough heat to survive the harsh Antarctic weather »

Discussion

Scientists spend money working out how to get down to lower and lower temperatures. Do you think it is important to continue to fund this work? Explain your answer.

Extra activities

1 a) Find out more about the different conditions that can be treated with cryosurgery.

   b) Are there any negative side effects that patients should be worried about?

WEBSITES

http://www.nobel.se/physics/educational/poster

http://www.ph.rhul.ac.uk/lowtemp/posters

Questions

1 What are the following temperatures when converted to the kelvin scale of temperature?
   - Room temperature 20°C
   - Human body temperature 37°C
   - The temperature of most of the universe −269°C
   - The temperature of liquid nitrogen −196°C
   - The surface of Triton, a moon of Neptune −238°C
   - The boiling point of water 100°C
   - The surface of the Sun 6000°C
   - The coldest temperature ever recorded on Earth.

2 What is a microkelvin?

3 Explain what the word 'superconductor' means.

4 What is a nebula?

5 When a normal star has used up all its hydrogen fuel, what happens next? How will this happen?

6 When our Sun dies, what is it likely to end up as?

7 When surgeons use cryosurgery, how does the liquid nitrogen work?

8 Why is cryosurgery such a good idea?

9 Explain how two different creatures have evolved to be able to live in very cold conditions.

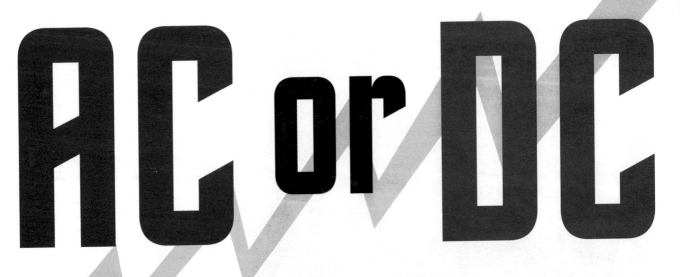

AC or DC

We take it for granted that school experiments use DC (direct current) power supplies but that household gadgets work on AC (alternating current). But that wouldn't be the case if Thomas Alva Edison had had his way.

« Edison was a prolific inventor – although many of his inventions were really made by people who worked for him »

AC and DC

DC stands for **direct current**. In DC the electrons (negatively charged particles) flow one way round the circuit only, from the negative terminal of the battery to the positive terminal. Unfortunately, we still have to talk about current flowing from positive to negative even though we know all about electrons. This is because scientists thought that some sort of fluid flowed round a circuit and they decided this fluid would go from positive to negative. The fluid was given the name 'current' because currents (of water, for example) flow. When the fluid flowed onto an object it was said to 'charge' the object. 'Charge' comes from the word for filling something. You still hear this old-fashioned word when someone says 'charge your glasses' meaning 'fill your glasses' with champagne for a toast at a wedding. The reason we use the letter I to stand for current comes from the French word for current, which is intensité.

AC stands for **alternating current**. In AC the electrons travel back and forth. In the UK we use 50 Hz AC. This means the current has a frequency of 50 hertz or that the electron flow goes back and forth 50 times per second.

Edison is best known for inventing the light bulb. It wasn't easy. He tried everything, including a whisker from his colleague's beard, to make a filament for his light bulb that didn't burn out after just a few minutes. Finally he succeeded by putting an inert gas inside the bulb. The tungsten filament lamps in many homes today are Edison's design.

But Edison was a very prolific inventor. He owned his own company which manufactured lamps, dynamos and motors based on his own patents. Life was certainly going Edison's way until, that is, a young man from Eastern Europe emigrated to the USA.

Nikola Tesla had worked for the Continental Edison Company in Paris where he had invented a motor driven by alternating current. He wanted to show the great man himself. But Edison laughed and told Tesla not to waste his time on alternating current.

Tesla was disappointed but, with a friend, he set up a small company making AC motors. Soon he became Edison's rival.

The big advantage of alternating current is that you can send it over long distances from the generator to the customer without it losing energy. This doesn't work with direct current – everyone has to have their own generator in their back yard (or quite close by).

Edison wanted everyone to buy DC motors and DC generators from him. If they chose AC then his company would go bust! He just had to persuade them that Tesla was wrong.

Edison even tried to show that AC was too dangerous to use by arranging the first execution by electric chair in New York State using alternating current. The press was there, waiting to witness the execution and waiting to report how dangerous alternating current was. The condemned man was brought in and strapped to the chair. The switch was thrown and the alternating current ran through his body. But it didn't kill him. Changes were made, the straps

Why does AC travel so well?

When the generating station transmits current to all its customers it has to make sure that enough energy arrives at each home to make all the appliances work. A lot of energy is wasted as heat as the current flows down the miles of cable before it gets to us. Any current flowing along a wire will make it heat up. Higher currents waste more energy in the form of heat than lower currents. To make sure that only the minimum amount of energy is lost, the current is reduced as low as possible for the journey. To do this engineers use transformers to 'step up' the voltage before it is transmitted and more transformers to 'step down' the voltage to a safe 230 volts at local substations before it is sent into peoples' homes. Stepping up the voltage has the effect of 'stepping down' the current and this is how they make sure that only a little energy is wasted.

The most important point is that transformers only work on AC. You can't step up or step down direct current. If we used direct current, as Edison wanted, we couldn't transmit it without wasting lots of energy on the way.

« Electric power is transmitted to customers at extremely high voltages (400 000 V typically). This is to keep the current as low as possible and save energy »

were tightened, and the switch was thrown. The condemned man's body tensed as the electric current made every muscle contract. But still he was alive. Again and again they tried and the smell of burning flesh began to fill

« The electric chair has never been a very efficient way of executing people. It tends to cook them rather than electrocute them »

the room. Finally, after several hours, the man died. But if it was supposed to prove the dangers of alternating current, it was a poor display!

But Tesla was clever. He discovered a strange phenomenon. The human body can conduct very high frequency alternating currents (current that flows back and forth thousands of times per second) without being affected. The current doesn't electrocute you because it doesn't

If it wasn't for Tesla the skyline of America would be very different.

penetrate the skin. It is conducted over your skin – the 'skin effect'. He even put on demonstrations where he would connect himself up to these high frequencies and light up a light bulb or melt a copper wire he was holding in his hand. This was the proof people needed to be convinced that AC was safe enough to be used in their homes and offices.

Edison just had to admit defeat. He still made lots of money running labs that turned out hundreds of inventions – but the

DC generator was just not one of his most successful inventions.

Unfortunately Tesla never really made any money out of his inventions – he had to sell all his patents to pay off other debts. As he grew older his inventions became more and more bizarre. He even considered beaming electricity from the USA to France to power the Paris World Fair and he had ideas about deathrays to

destroy planes at distances of hundreds of kilometres.

However, one thing is certain. If it weren't for Tesla the skyline of America would be very different. The skyscrapers of any city just wouldn't be so high if we still relied upon DC, because the direct current would lose so much energy on its way from the generator in the basement to the rooms on the upper floors. ■

Questions

1 What is the difference between DC and AC?

2 Energy is wasted when electric current is transmitted to our homes. How does this happen? What do engineers do to make sure that the amount of energy wasted is as low as possible?

3 What difference does it make to our lives today that we use AC rather than DC in our homes?

4 How did Edison try to prove that AC was dangerous?

5 How did Tesla demonstrate that AC was safe? Why might we accuse Tesla of cheating a bit in his demonstration?

Extra activities

1 Find out what forms of energy are used to generate electricity in
   a) power stations in the UK, and
   b) the power station nearest to your home.

2 Tesla had the idea of beaming electricity to France. Today the UK imports electricity from France via a link under the channel. Find out what this link is called and what proportion of our electricity we import.

The luminiferous ether
or how scientists got it wrong

Since the time of the ancient Greeks, scientists have tried to understand what light is made of. Pythagoras, in the 6th century BC, suggested it was a stream of bits called light particles. This explained perfectly how shadows were made by the light particles travelling in straight lines past an object.

« The ancient Greeks thought light was a stream of particles »

But by the 17th century, the idea of light particles was out of fashion for most scientists. Sir Isaac Newton still believed that light was made of particles (he called them corpuscles). He also thought that the light corpuscles came out of our eyes when we looked at an object – a bit like the X-rays out of Superman's eyes when he uses his X-ray vision. Newton was obviously wrong because we should be able to see in the dark if the corpuscles came from our eyes. Superman's X-ray vision is also wrong. If his eyes give out X-rays, he would have no way of capturing the X-rays on the other side of the object to see what was inside it!

ISAAC NEWTON 1642–1727

At school Newton was always at the bottom of the class. But he loved to read and this is what started him thinking about the world around him. He bought a prism from a travelling fair and worked out how to split white light into its colours. He was such a superstitious man that he was convinced a rainbow must be magical as it was mentioned in the Old Testament of the Bible. He insisted the rainbow had seven colours because be believed that seven was a magic number. To this day people are still uncertain what colour indigo is.

« Isaac Newton is most famous for his work on gravity, but he also thought a lot about what light was made of »

At about this time another famous scientist from Holland, called Huygens, described light travelling along like the waves along a string or waves on the surface of water. Huygens' description of 'light waves' explained reflection and refraction perfectly and most scientists agreed with his ideas.

But there was a problem with Huygens' idea of light waves. They needed something to travel in, like water waves travel on the surface of the water or sound in the air.

Despite this problem, scientists continued to believe in the ether

To solve this problem scientists decided that the whole of space was filled with a special substance called 'the luminiferous ether'. Light waves were supposed to travel through this 'ether' to get from the Sun or stars to the Earth.

But even this idea caused difficulties. They knew that the speed of light was very high – more than a hundred thousand miles per second! They also knew that waves travelled fastest along very tight, springy wires. How could the ether be springy enough for the light to travel that fast **but**, at the same time, be thin enough for the Earth and the other planets to travel through it for years without slowing down?

Despite this problem, scientists continued to believe in the ether and spent many hours trying to measure how fast the Earth was travelling through the ether.

The most famous experiment was done by a brilliant young scientist called Michelson (he was the first American to be awarded a Nobel Prize for science). He set up some apparatus which sent two light beams in different directions at right angles to each other.

If the Earth is travelling through the ether then there must be an 'ether wind' blowing past the apparatus. Light travelling in one direction is aiming into the ether wind, light in another direction would be travelling across the ether wind.

Michelson decided that the two beams of light would feel different effects because of this ether wind. So the two beams of light would travel at different speeds and arrive at the final telescope at different times. His apparatus was designed to create a particular pattern from the two light beams (called an interference pattern) when they arrived at the telescope.

Then he turned the whole apparatus round by 90° to see what pattern he got. He was expecting the two patterns to be

Light is always described as a transverse, electromagnetic wave. Transverse means the amplitude is at right angles to the direction the light is travelling. Electromagnetic waves can travel through a vacuum where they always travel at the same speed, 300 000 000 m/s.

When light hits a reflective surface it is reflected at the same angle as the angle of incidence.

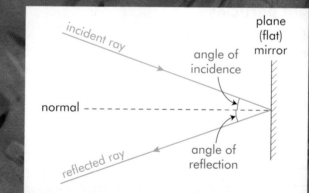

« When light is reflected, angle of incidence = angle of reflection »

When light tries to go through a transparent material, like glass, it slows down. One effect of this is refraction. If the light hits the glass surface at an angle to the normal it will be bent on its way in and bent again on its way out.

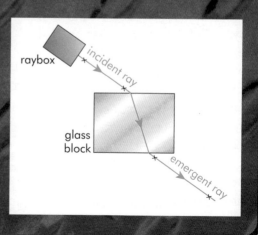

« Michelson's experiment was supposed to work out what happened to light as the Earth flew through the 'ether'. In the end, scientists had to admit they were wrong and agreed that the ether did not exist »

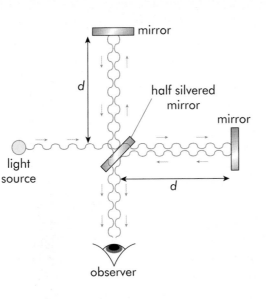

showed that the ether did not exist. Finally scientists had to admit that they had got it wrong and decided to look for another way of describing the way light travels through the vacuum that surrounds the Earth.

Michelson was forced to conclude that: 'the result of the hypothesis of the stationary ether is thus shown to be incorrect.'

Something very important came from all these experiments. They led to Einstein's famous 'special theory of relativity' and to our present-day model of light as both a wave **and** a flow of particles, called 'photons'. Who said you can't have it both ways? ■

different because of the direction in which the ether wind was blowing. But it didn't matter how carefully he did the experiment, he could get no differences at all.

Another scientist, Lorentz, from Holland came up with an ingenious explanation to try to solve Michelson's problem. He suggested that any object travelling along the 'ether wind' physically contracted (got shorter!) while an object travelling across the ether wind would have no effect. This would explain perfectly

why Michelson got no changes in his interference pattern.

In the end every experiment designed to measure the speed of the Earth through the ether

Questions

1. Newton believed that our eyes gave out light corpuscles so that we could see. Explain why it is obvious that this idea is incorrect.

2. Huygens had a different idea about light. What was Huygens' idea about light and why did it seem to work perfectly at first?

3. Draw a diagram to show what happens to a beam of light when it is refracted. Why does this happen to light beams?

4. There was a problem with Huygens' idea about light. What was this problem?

5. Scientists came up with the idea of the 'luminiferous ether' to solve their problem. What was the luminiferous ether?

6. There was even a problem with the ether idea? What was it?

7. Michaelson eventually decided that the ether idea was wrong. What made him come to this conclusion?

« Michelson tried everything he could think of to measure how fast the Earth travelled through the ether »

Extra activities

1. Light is now known to be an electromagnetic wave. James Clerk Maxwell was the first person to come up with this idea. Find out about Maxwell and what the term 'electromagnetic' actually means.

2. We now think that light is made up of particles called photons. Find out who came up with the idea of photons.

Jocelyn Bell was studying for a PhD in astronomy at Cambridge University in 1967 when she spotted some strange signals from one part of the sky. They were short wavelength radio waves 3.7 m long and they came in very regular bursts – every 1.3373 seconds. They were certainly different from the signal astronomers usually found coming from stars and galaxies. Jocelyn and her supervisor Antony Hewish, couldn't work out what the signals were, so they jokingly called them LGM1, for little green men!

« Jocelyn Bell Burnell discovered the first pulsar – but missed out on the Nobel Prize »

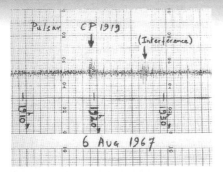

« Jocelyn noticed these signals from a pulsar for the first time in August 1967 »

Still confused by the signals, Jocelyn looked at a different part of the sky, and to her amazement found another pulsing signal. This time it was pulsing every 1.2 seconds. It now seemed very unlikely that it was a signal from extraterrestrial beings. But what was it?

Jocelyn and Antony announced their discovery and asked if anyone could come up with an explanation for what it was. The obvious answer was that it came from a spinning neutron star. Scientists had predicted that extremely large stars would be destroyed in a supernova explosion and collapse in on themselves at the end of their lives. They form incredibly dense material where the gravity is so strong that the protons and electrons are forced together to form neutrons. They are therefore called neutron stars. Only neutron stars could possibly be small and dense enough to spin this fast and give out signals every second. It seemed likely that Jocelyn's observation was the first evidence that this really happened.

The pulsing star became known as a pulsar and they changed the name of the signal from LGM1 to CP1 (for Cambridge Pulsar).

Perhaps unfairly, Antony Hewish was awarded the Nobel Prize in 1974 for the discovery of the pulsar, even though Jocelyn Bell was the first person to spot the signals.

By 1993, pulsars were back in the news when two more astronomers were awarded the Nobel Prize for discovering a new type of pulsar. Joseph Taylor and Russell Hulse discovered a binary pulsar (two neutron stars that orbit each other).

« Antony Hewish was awarded the Nobel Prize in 1974 for the discovery of the pulsar »

Radio waves and pulsars

Radio waves are long wavelength electromagnetic waves. On Earth they are used to transmit radio and television programmes. Very short wavelength radio waves (or microwaves) are used to carry mobile phone messages.

A pulsar is a very special neutron star that spins very rapidly and gives out sharp pulses of radio waves as it spins.

A neutron star is formed when a heavy star gets towards the end of its life. Usually a star will run out of fuel (hydrogen) and start using its helium as fuel. It fuses the helium nuclei into heavier elements. As it does this it expands into a red giant. Then when it gets to the end of its fuel supply it collapses and forms a white dwarf. Heavier stars collapse too but much more violently! They become so dense that all the protons and electrons get close together and form neutrons. This matter is so dense that a teaspoon would weigh 100 million tonnes! The outer layers of the exploding star are thrown outwards as a

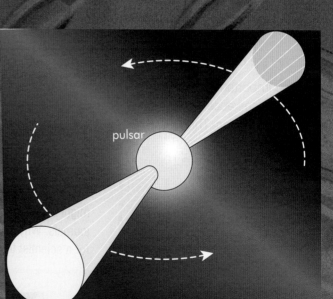

pulsar

« Pulsars are extremely dense neutron stars that spin and give out pulses of radio waves »

supernova (star explosion). The neutron stars are small enough to be able to spin at the very high speeds needed to send out pulses every second or so – as Jocelyn Bell saw in her observations of the first pulsar.

Hulse had noticed that the pulses from one pulsar were irregular. His idea was that there were two stars orbiting each other very rapidly – about once every eight hours! This is quite a speed as each star was about 1.4 times as heavy as our Sun, though much, much smaller due to their high density – only about 20 kilometres diameter! They were about as far apart as our Earth and Moon.

The reason the scientific world became so excited by the discovery of a binary pulsar is that it could be the perfect way to test Einstein's famous General Theory of Relativity. In 1916, Einstein suggested two important ideas. Firstly that time and space are linked to form 'space-time'. Gravity is no longer a force. Instead heavy objects curve space around themselves. A planet like the Earth only orbits the Sun because space around the Sun is curved and it is the only way the Earth can go.

The second important idea was that when masses accelerate, they give out gravity waves. This is like electrons accelerating up and down an aerial and giving out radio waves. Unfortunately as yet, we haven't found a way to detect gravity waves – if indeed they exist.

Taylor and Hulse's binary pulsar may be just what the scientists have been waiting for. The two neutron stars are moving so fast they should be emitting huge amounts of gravity waves. This should mean they are losing energy and slowing down. Astronomers have been observing them since their discovery – and they seem to have slowed down.

Now scientists are planning to build instruments that should be able to detect gravitational radiation directly on Earth. ■

« Joseph Taylor and Russell Hulse were awarded the Nobel Prize in 1993 for discovering the binary pulsar »

Questions

1 Why did Jocelyn and Antony give their signals the code LGM1?

2 Jocelyn soon had to change the code to CP1. What does this stand for and why did she change the code?

3 Explain what a neutron star is. How is it different from a white dwarf?

4 How do we know a pulsar is spinning very fast?

5 How did Hulse work out he had seen two pulsars orbiting round each other?

6 Explain why Taylor and Hulse's observations are so important and why they could be very useful in the future.

7 In both cases in this article the scientists told colleagues about their discoveries. Jocelyn and Antony asked for ideas about what their signals might be and both groups published their findings in important scientific journals. Why do scientists collaborate like this and why is it important for a scientist to get his/her work published in a journal?

« The theory that space-time is curved can be tested using observations of a binary pulsar »

Extra activities

Chinese astronomers first observed the Crab Nebula as an intense explosion in AD1054. Find out more about the Crab Nebula and whether it has a pulsar at its centre.

@ WEBSITES @

http://www.nobel.se

KIRN AKRAM

CERTIFIED MOON ROCK HANDLER

« Kirn Akram is a physics student with a particular interest in Moon rocks »

Kirn Akram is a physics student at the University of Reading. She has two claims to fame – she has seen a Space Shuttle launch live and she is certified to handle lunar rocks. This is her story:

❝ *In 1998, I was given a Millennium Award for my work in my local community. I had been a peer motivator for two years at the Slough Summer University, helping local young people.*

I had to decide what to do with the money and finally decided to visit NASA to find out about the different types of educational facilities that they provide for young people aged between 14 and 21. They run a whole range of student programmes, including the Sharp Programme, the Coop Programme, space flight opportunities and Design a Mission to Mars Programme, to name but a few.

I spent about eight months organising the trip. While I was there I visited the Neutral Buoyancy Centre. It is the largest indoor swimming pool in the world where astronauts learn space walking techniques. At Ellington Field I saw the space shuttle training aircraft – the 'Gulfstream Jet Trainer' – which

« The control room at NASA »

is modified to behave like the Space Shuttle during landing, and I saw the Boeing 747 aircraft that transports the Space Shuttle fleet around the US. I found out from NASA astronauts and engineers all about the International Space Station – the largest and most ambitious project at the Johnson Space Centre in Texas – and about their ideas for future missions to the Moon and Mars.

Everything I saw was absolutely amazing, but the highlight had to be the launch of the Atlantis STS 106 Space Shuttle on 8th September 2000. I had VIP front seat passes along with the astronauts' families and NASA authorities. Not many people get to view a live launch – not even people who have worked at NASA for years! I could almost feel the force of the launch go right through me. I'm proud that I saw launch number 99 of the 100 Space Shuttle launches listed on a commemorative poster produced by NASA.

Since then I have organised an interactive space science course – 'Shooting into Orbit: A Journey to NASA and Beyond' – for people between 14 and 21, as part of the Tower Hamlets Summer University. Because of this, NASA agreed that I could go back in 2001, work as a student volunteer and take part in their Education Workshops programme at NASA's Jet Propulsion Laboratory in Pasadena. It was there that I became certified to handle lunar rocks.

At the moment I am working on ordering the lunar rocks from NASA (which are worth $25 billion) so that I can include them in my next space science courses. 99 ■

« To see a Space Shuttle launch is a great honour »

Extra activities

1 Find out what NASA stands for and what facilities they have for members of the public and for school groups.

2 The US government spends a lot of money on public and school-based activities at NASA, including lots of free gifts for schoolteachers. At CERN (the international particle physics laboratories) in Switzerland they also offer guided tours and free gifts. In the UK, places like Sellafield offer guided tours and free teaching materials. Why do you think governments spend money on public events at places like this?

@ WEBSITES @

http://www.NASA.gov

Is there a future for scientists in space?

It is over 40 years since the first manned space flight. Edwin Cartlidge is a journalist for the magazine *Physics World*. He explores the costs and benefits of sending humans into space.

« Edwin Cartlidge did a degree in physics before becoming a journalist »

There have been long arguments about whether it is a good idea to send humans into space. Some people think that exploring space should be left to robots. They point out that there have already been many unmanned space probes that have made many discoveries – and they are far less expensive than sending humans into space. Other people think that only humans can make important discoveries in astronomy and planetary science by setting foot on other planets.

Value for money?

The high costs of launching spacecraft means that only a few people have gone further than low Earth orbit. Even the most modest manned mission to Mars would cost between $25 and $50 billion. Andrew Coates of the Mullard Space Science laboratory at University College, London believes that robots are a 'realistic, useful and inspirational' scientific programme in space. He points out that missions with unmanned probes, which cost only about $100million to $1billion, have been sent to every planet except Pluto. They have landed on Mars and Venus. They have flown past comets and have rendezvoused with an asteroid. They have probed Jupiter's atmosphere and have studied the distant universe.

People in favour of human space flight argue that only humans have the judgement and flexibility to carry out detailed studies on other planets. 'A human return to the Moon will be a boon to science,' says Paul Spudis of the Lunar and Planetary Institute in Houston, Texas. Spudis argues that by studying the geology of the Moon, we can learn about the processes that shaped all of our neighbouring planets. He also points out that the

Moon offers astronomers an excellent place to observe the rest of the universe as it has no atmosphere to block out light or radio waves. Spudis also says that the far side of the Moon is the only place in our Solar System that does not receive radio pollution from the Earth.

The human touch

Spudis agrees that robots are good but he believes that human intelligence and flexibility are needed to solve many scientific problems. He adds that only humans are able to maintain and repair equipment in space.

Like the Moon, Mars is rich in geology. Recent pictures from the Mars Global Surveyor showed layers of rock similar to sedimentary rocks on Earth. This may be evidence that there was liquid water on the red planet. There was also some evidence of primitive life in a meteorite that came from Mars. 'But probes (such as Europe's Beagle II, that is scheduled to land on Mars in the near future) will only scratch the planet's surface and may not find evidence of life,' says Julian Hiscox of Reading University. He believes that, to hunt for signs of life, humans must go to Mars, armed with drills and rock hammers. 'Contrary to what most people think, human exploration of Mars is not impossible. Although it is very risky, the cost of several missions to Mars is less than the total cost of the International Space Station,' adds Hiscox.

However, Coates believes that problems with the development of reusable launch vehicles will keep the cost of sending humans into

« Sending astronauts into space is costly – but is it worth the money? »

space too high for some time. He adds that the human body is not suited to life in space because of the effects of low gravity, which weakens bones, and muscles, and the effects of solar and cosmic radiation.

Spudis, on the other hand, points to human fascination for seeing new places with their own eyes: 'I think this is a good thing and it has served us well in the past.' ∎

« Sending robots into space is cheaper and safer – but are they as good? »

Extra activities

1 Write an article based upon the one you have just read, arguing strongly either for sending people into space or for sending robots into space. Make sure you put your case forward clearly and include all the points to support your arguments.

2 Look back at your article and compare it with the one Edwin wrote. He tries to be very balanced and to put both sides of the argument. How is yours different? What sort of language did you use? Did you leave out any facts or exaggerate anything to put your case more strongly?

3 Often newspapers are accused of being biased in the way they report science stories. For example, they may talk about 'Frankenstein Foods' or 'Scientists Playing God'. Do you think newspapers should be balanced in their reporting? Do you think they are indeed balanced in their reporting?

In the battle of Trafalgar an amputated leg would be cauterised by dipping the severed end in hot tar. Other wounds would be cauterised by applying red-hot irons direct to the wound. Amputation at that time was a tricky business with no anaesthetic and no antibiotics. The main aim was to remove the limb as fast as possible and use every trick in the book to stop the massive blood loss. Indeed there was one surgeon who was famous for the speed of amputations – he could remove a whole leg in just a few seconds. Records show, however, that during one operation he successfully removed the patient's leg at thigh level but also cut off one of the patient's testicles and two fingers from his assistant's hand!

Little

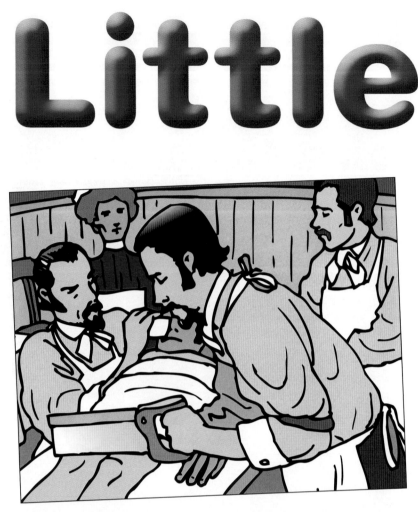

« The trick was to cut the patient's leg off before they died from shock or excessive blood loss »

Doing it with light

Thankfully we have come a long way since then, but blood loss is still a major problem during operations. The old fashioned way is to tie off the ends of the blood vessels with stitches. Nowadays a

A laser is a highly concentrated beam of light. Unlike normal light beams it doesn't spread out as it travels so it can be directed very accurately onto one spot. The laser energy is so concentrated that it builds up heat in the object. This means lasers can be used to cut through sheet metal. In surgery, a laser will burn rapidly through a patient's flesh in the same way. Lasers are also used to weld a patient's retina onto the back of their eye when it becomes detached.

surgeon can use an electric current or even a laser to stop the bleeding. In fact a surgeon can use a laser both to cut into the patient's flesh and to cauterise the blood vessels at the same time. The heat causes the blood vessels to shrink and a blood clot to form until the blood stops flowing.

Unfortunately lasers and electric currents only work near to the surface – they penetrate to only about 2 millimetres. If a patient has been in an accident and has internal bleeding lasers won't help. Blood loss from internal haemorrhaging is the real killer in road accidents.

bleeders

Doing it with sound

Recently scientists have discovered that they can use sound to treat bleeding.

One particularly clever device is called a harmonic scalpel. During an operation the surgeon simply holds the device against the bleeding. The harmonic scalpel gives out ultrasound at 55 kHz. As the scalpel vibrates against the damaged blood vessels, friction causes the temperature to rise and this cauterises the wound. Of course this only works where the harmonic scalpel is in direct contact with the wound.

Now high-frequency ultrasound up to 10 MHz is being investigated as

a way to stop internal bleeding. The biggest advantage of this technique is that it could be applied by paramedics at the scene of an accident, to stabilise a patient before transfer to hospital.

Ultrasound can penetrate tissue and will cauterise blood vessels deep within the body. The surgeon has to focus high-energy ultrasound waves to a point inside the body. The power of the

> ### Units
>
> The unit of frequency is the hertz (Hz). A frequency of 15 000 hertz means the vibrations happen at a rate of 15 000 per second.
>
> The unit of power is the watt (W). A power of 1 watt means that 1 joule of energy arrives per second.
>
> The unit of pressure is the pascal (Pa). A pressure of 1 pascal is exerted if a force of 1 newton rests on an area of 1 m^2. 1 MPa is 1 megapascal, which means 1 million pascals.

« For road accident victims internal bleeding from their injuries is the greatest killer. The ambulance teams can do nothing to stop internal bleeding »

> Ultrasound is very high frequency sound that is above the normal range of human hearing. Humans typically can hear to about 20 000 Hz but by the age of 15 the best they can do is often as low as 15 000 Hz – and this gets worse as we get older and if our hearing is damaged by loud sounds. In hospitals, ultrasound is most often used to scan a pregnant woman's abdomen to produce an image of the fetus in the uterus.

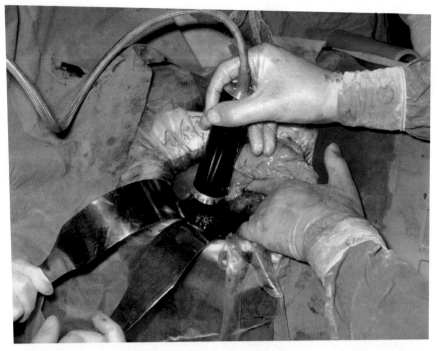

« The high frequency sound heats up the blood vessels by friction and makes them stop bleeding »

ultrasound waves is between 1000 and 10 000 W/cm^2. This is very much higher than the ultrasound waves that are used to image the developing fetus during an ultrasound scan. There doctors use less than 1 W/cm^2. The high power ultrasound waves hit the damaged tissue and exert a pressure of about 1 MPa. As the tissue absorbs the energy in the waves, its temperature rises to over 70°C. This is enough to destroy the blood vessels and this stops the bleeding. Healthy tissue nearby is completely unaffected because the ultrasound beam is accurately focused on the damaged tissue and not elsewhere.

In the future if surgeons can focus the ultrasound beam accurately enough they may be able to cut off the blood flow to a tumour and kill it. Already ultrasound is used to treat prostate cancer. Doctors are undertaking trials to see if it can be used on breast tumours or cancer of the liver or kidneys without the need for invasive surgery. ■

Extra activities

Find out what other uses there are for ultrasound.

Discussion

Recent research indicates that ultrasound scans on unborn babies may have long-term effects. Find out what these effects are. Do you think that the benefits of a scan outweigh the possible risks, and that, therefore, all pregnant women should have a scan?

Questions

1 Why are lasers and electric currents unable to control internal bleeding?

2 Why are doctors keen to find ways to control internal bleeding?

3 Scientists have found ways to use ultrasound to control bleeding.
   a) Explain what ultrasound is.
   b) How is the ultrasound that is used for scanning pregnant women different from the ultrasound used to control bleeding?

4 The ultrasound exerts a pressure of 1 MPa.
   a) How many newtons of force would it take on an area of 1 m^2 to exert a pressure of 1 MPa?
   b) How many newtons of force would it take to exert a pressure of 1 MPa on an area of 1 cm^2?

5 If the power of the ultrasound is 10 000 W/cm^2,
   a) how many joules of energy would be sent into 1 cm^2 of the body in 3 seconds?
   b) how many seconds should the surgeon hold the ultrasound probe in place if he/she needs to deliver 50 kJ of energy to the wound?

6 If body tissue rises from body temperature of 37°C to 70°C in 3 seconds, what is the rate of temperature rise per second?

7 The ultrasound in a harmonic scalpel is noted as 55 kHz. What does 55 kHz stand for? How can you tell it is ultrasound from this information?

8 How does the harmonic scalpel generate the heat that causes the wound to stop bleeding?

The sky is falling

There are now around 100 000 objects in orbit around the Earth. Some are only the size of a large coin, others are full size working satellites. Many are the remains of the 3800 rocket launches that have happened since the launch of the first artificial Earth satellite, Sputnik, in 1957. One of these objects re-enters the Earth's atmosphere every week. Fortunately most burn up entirely, as they speed through the upper atmosphere due to the friction between the spacecraft and the air. Some of the larger objects do not and they have to be tracked very carefully to make sure that they are unlikely to cause injury or damage to buildings.

The biggest problem now is that these pieces of space debris may collide with working satellites and cause damage. In fact the French satellite, CERISE, is famous for being the first working satellite to be damaged by a collision. Its stabilisation boom was cut off by a piece of debris from an Ariane rocket when they collided at 50 000 km/h. This vapourised CERISE's boom and sent the satellite into an uncontrolled spin. It took engineers at the ground station a lot of effort to locate the satellite and re-stabilise it so that it could continue to send information back to mission control.

« There are thousands of objects in orbit around the Earth. Some are even still working! »

Earth. Some polar orbiting satellites are in Low-Earth Orbit (LEO) at an altitude of between 200 km and 2000 km. They take only about 100 minutes to orbit from pole to pole and can observe the whole of the Earth in a day. These satellites can observe anything from land use to freak weather conditions, sea temperatures or military airports. Some of these satellites are only a few kilograms in mass and have a volume no larger than a football. These so-called nanosatellites do not even need a rocket to launch them into space. Old intercontinental ballistic missile launchers will do.

Even the Space Shuttle has had problems. While it was on its mission to repair the Hubble Telescope, it had a near miss with a piece of debris from a rocket. In fact the Space Shuttle has had to swerve a number of times to avoid collision.

There are about 5000 operational spacecraft in orbit around the

It is gravity that keeps a satellite in orbit around the Earth. Gravity is the force that keeps all objects in orbit around their parent including the planets and comets that orbit stars. Most planets have orbits that are approximately circular, but comets have strangely elliptical orbits, which means they take a very long time to complete one orbit. Any force towards the centre of a circle is called the centripetal force. For orbiting bodies, gravity provides the centripetal force.

« Modern satellites are so small that intercontinental ballistic missile launchers can launch them »

For a long time people in Europe believed that the Earth was the centre of the universe and that all planets and the Sun orbited around us, because this was how it was described in The Bible. People in the Arab world were far better informed. Only when Copernicus in the 16th century and Galileo in the 17th century had the courage to suggest that the Sun was at the centre of our Solar System did people in Europe start to re-think their ideas. However, it took a long time for people to come to terms with Galileo's suggestions. The influence of the Church and The Bible were so strong in medieval Europe that people could not possibly consider that they may be wrong. In fact, Galileo was imprisoned for years by the Church for daring to suggest that The Bible was wrong.

The satellites that are used for television transmission and phone calls are geostationary satellites. There are fewer of these (around 700 at the last count) and they orbit about six times further out than the radius of the Earth (36 000 km above the Earth). This part of the sky is not so densely populated so the risk of collision is much less. These satellites take much longer to orbit the Earth (24 hours or one complete Earth day) which makes sure that they remain above the same spot as seen from the Earth. They still travel quite fast though, typically 3100 m/s. At this speed they cover about 250 million metres per day just to keep up with the Earth.

NASA tracks the larger satellites and pieces of debris. It uses radar and telescopes to track more than 8500 objects orbiting the Earth. However SNAP, a microsatellite from Surrey Satellite Centre in Guildford, made the headlines when it successfully photographed another satellite while in orbit. The experts at NASA were not pleased

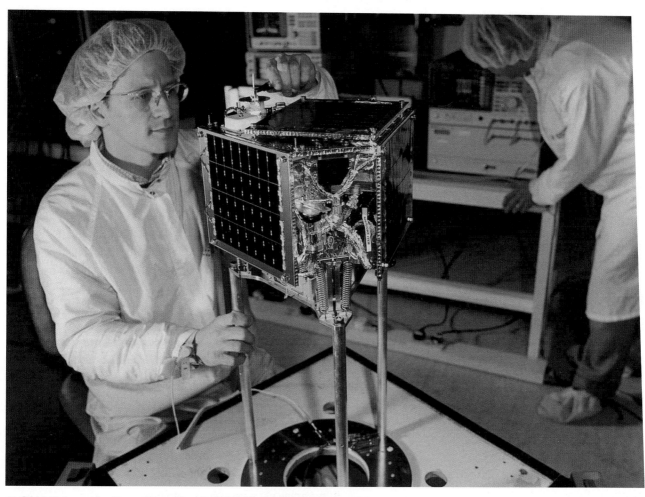

« SNAP is only the size of a football yet it managed to photograph important NASA satellites while in orbit »

when they realised what had happened.

Even astronomers are becoming annoyed by all the space debris. While they are observing far distant astronomical objects they find the long exposure photographic images are spoilt by trails of debris.

Soon they risk colliding with their active sister satellites

Scientists are now getting together to work out what they should do to control all this space debris. The problem will not go away and it's just not feasible to do a clean up in space. Worn-out geostationary satellites are sent into 'graveyard orbit' further away from the Earth. Larger fragments in LEO are controlled to re-enter the atmosphere where they will burn up. Unfortunately it's the smaller fragments, which cannot be tracked or controlled, that now pose a real problem.

Even more worrying is what is happening to defunct GPS (Global Positioning System) Satellites. They are sent to a 'grave yard orbit' about 500 km above the active GPS satellites' orbits of 14 000 km. After satellites are sent to this higher orbit all the remaining fuel is dumped so that there's no risk of explosion if they do collide.

It now seems that the Sun and Moon's gravity affect their orbit after a while making it more elliptical. Soon they risk colliding with their active sister satellites.

There is nothing the controllers can do about them.

With no fuel, the satellite cannot be moved. It is just a matter of time before they end up in the GPS operating zone where they pose a real threat to the whole Global Positioning System. Engineers are now working on ways to avert this disaster. ∎

Questions

1 What can geostationary satellites do that polar satellites cannot do? Explain why.

2 Some satellites are describes as LEO satellites. What does this stand for and why do they have this name?

3 Why does NASA bother to track 8500 orbiting objects when many of them are no longer operational?

4 Orbiting objects do not remain in orbit forever. What can happen to them at the end of their useful life?

5 If an LEO satellite is 700 km above the Earth and the Earth's radius is 6400 km, what is the radius of the satellite's orbit?

6 If an LEO satellite takes 100 minutes to orbit the Earth once, what speed is it travelling at?

7 CERISE was travelling at 50 000 km/h when it collided with some space debris and its stabilisation boom was cut off. Do you think the radius of its orbit is more or less than the one described in question 5? Explain your answer.

Discussion

All countries want their own satellites and it is now possible to buy them 'off the shelf'. Most of these countries are interested in polar orbiting satellites to monitor what's happening in their own country and in their neighbours'. Even quite poor countries will spend millions of dollars on satellite technology. On balance, do you think that the development of satellite technology has been to the benefit of humankind? Discuss this in your class.

Extra activities

There have been amazing advances in satellite technology since the first satellite was launched in 1957. Find out what satellites are used for.

WEBSITES

http://www.ph.surrey.ac.uk/satellites

JESSICA CHEUNG

Jessica has never been the type to take the easy way out. 'I've always chosen things that were difficult – a bit of a challenge. I always think, "I'm going to crack this!"'

《 Jessica Cheung – looking for the next challenge 》

Jessica is 25 and she's almost at the end of her PhD in physics. When she completes it she will earn the title Dr Cheung. Yet when she was at school it was not obvious what she should choose to do.

66 *Physics at school was a struggle but I was determined to meet the challenge. My best subjects at GCSE were French, Art and Latin but I was told by my careers advisor that Physics and Maths would open more doors for me in the future, so I took A-levels in Maths, Physics, Chemistry and Art. Then I decided that a degree in physics with French would be a challenge as it involved a year studying physics in France alongside French students. It was hard work but I came back able to speak French fluently and able to understand the physics in England better.* 99

After a year doing an MSc in applied optics, Jessica was

At university a physics student will take a three year BSc (Bachelor of Science) or a four year MPhys (Master in Physics) or MSci (Master in Science) degree. The main difference is that during the fourth year you study your chosen topics in greater depth and learn how scientists really undertake research. People who want to work in research usually take the four-year option.

The top students will be awarded a First Class Honours degree. Those who do very well will be awarded an Upper Second Class Honours degree (usually abbreviated to 2i or two-one).

Below this is a Lower Second Class Honours degree (or 2ii or two-two). Finally there's a Third Class Honours degree. For those who do poorly there's the possibility of being awarded a Pass degree.

After your undergraduate degree you can do a postgraduate degree. This is either a one-year Masters degree (MSc) or a three-year Doctor of Philosophy (even though it's in Physics!) (PhD).

An MSc is usually aimed at a particular area of work, such as medical physics or optics. You can take this if you pass a BSc or MPhys with a 2i degree or better. Students who want to get a doctorate (PhD) have to work for three more years after their first degree. During this time they have a personal project which they work on alone, but with a lot of support and advice from their personal supervisor. Their supervisor has a particular interest in the topic of their research, as it's an area where they also have particular expertise.

I use beams of neutrons and fire them at the silicon crystals.

offered a place to study for a PhD. This involves three years on her own research project where she will become a real expert in her topic and discover things no one else knows.

❝ *I'm working on neutron scattering as a way of finding out about the oxygen you get when you are growing silicon crystals for the electronics industry. Normally*

Neutrons are neutral particles with almost the same mass as a proton. They are found in the nucleus of atoms. Scientists use them a lot in experiments because they can be fired at materials. This might make the material change in some way or might cause it to become radioactive. Then the atoms may break apart or neutrons may be scattered by the substance. Scientists call this effect diffraction though it's not quite the same as when waves are diffracted by going through a small gap or past an obstacle. The patterns that the neutrons make as they are scattered can be used to work out how the atoms are arranged in the material.

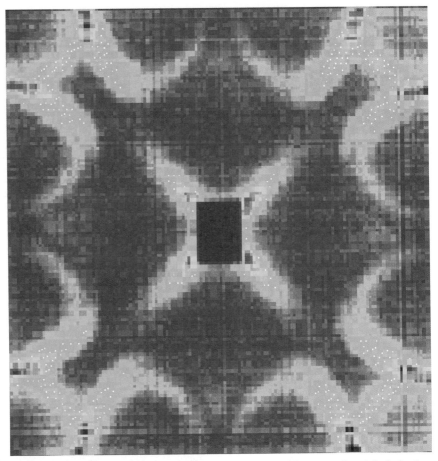

≪ **Small angle neutron scattering from silicon – the trick is to interpret what these patterns mean** ≫

the electronics industry wants absolutely perfect silicon crystals for making silicon chips (the integrated circuits in all electronic devices). Unfortunately, you always get some oxygen which forms silicon dioxide in the silicon. It seems that silicon dioxide can be quite useful inside the silicon as it can act as a 'getter'. For example, if some iron impurities come along we don't want it to contaminate the surface of the silicon. The silicon dioxide will grab the iron impurities and take them away from the surface, leaving the surface perfectly clean for the electronic devices to be formed on it.

What I'm doing is seeing how the silicon dioxide grows in the silicon crystal. I use beams of neutrons and fire them at the silicon crystals. As they go through they are

diffracted. I choose neutrons of just the right speed to make sure they are diffracted by the silicon dioxide in the crystal. When the neutrons come out the other side, they form a pattern, which I have to interpret to work out the average size of the silicon dioxide particles. They are typically about 500 nm across (0.000 000 5 m or 0.0005 mm). Then the question is, can we make the silicon dioxide particles bigger or smaller by heat-treating the silicon? One thing I have discovered is that if I heat the silicon for 3000 hours the bigger silicon dioxide particles seem to eat the smaller ones. I'm not sure why, yet.

All the results from experiments over forty years can be put onto one graph to see how they *compare. So far it has been possible to draw a straight line through all the results for high temperatures and low temperatures. The problem has always been in the middle. There are some very strange results here which no one can explain. This is the range of temperature we are working on. It's interesting that our results lie much closer to the straight line than anyone else's **and** we can explain why. It's really good when things work out as you predicted.* 99

As Jessica comes to the end of her studies it's interesting to look back on the amazing experiences she's had.

66 *One of my most memorable experiences was a 6 week Summer School in Grenoble in France. We all had to produce posters about our work to share our ideas with everyone else. I met other students from all over the world and they were all so friendly. In fact I often go to conferences and meetings in different parts of the world and what's surprising is that there's a real sense of community – everyone knows everyone else and you soon get talking to people and hear about huge projects where people from several countries are collaborating.* 99

So what is Jessica looking forward to as she finishes her PhD?

66 *The first thing is the graduation ceremony. My parents are from China. They lived there during the cultural revolution. They both had to leave school at the age of 12. They are pleased that I am getting the chance of a good education. They are really looking forward to the graduation ceremony. After that I haven't really decided yet. But I'm sure it will be a challenge.* 99 ∎

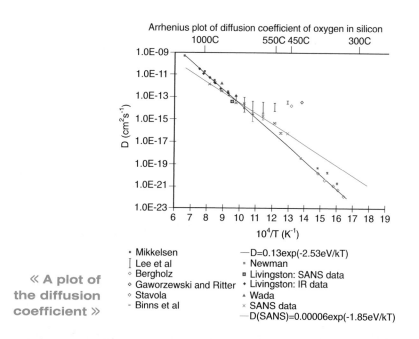

« A plot of the diffusion coefficient »

- Mikkelsen
- Lee et al
- Bergholz
- Gaworzewski and Ritter
- Stavola
- Binns et al
— D=0.13exp(-2.53eV/kT)
- Newman
- Livingston: SANS data
- Livingston: IR data
- Wada
× SANS data
— D(SANS)=0.00006exp(-1.85eV/kT)

Questions

1 Jessica talks about neutron scattering. What is a neutron?

2 Scientists like neutrons because they can be fired at materials. What might happen when neutrons are fired at different materials?

3 How does Jessica use her neutrons?

4 Why is the electronic industry interested in working out how to make perfect silicon chips?

5 Why is the silicon dioxide useful when it is in the silicon?

6 Jessica is trying to find out whether she can make the silicon dioxide particles bigger or smaller. What has she found happens after she has heated the silicon for 3000 hours? Has she worked out why this happens yet?

7 Jessica says it feels good when things work out as you have predicted. Why is it important to make predictions when you are doing an experiment?

8 Jessica also talks about making posters and sharing ideas with everyone else. Why is it important for scientists to do this?

Extra activities

If you go to the research pages of any university physics department you will find out what particular projects they are doing there. Often they will include copies of posters that students have done recently. Look at these and then make a poster in the same way about one of your experiments.

@ WEBSITES @

www.ill.Fr

www.isis.rl.ac.uk

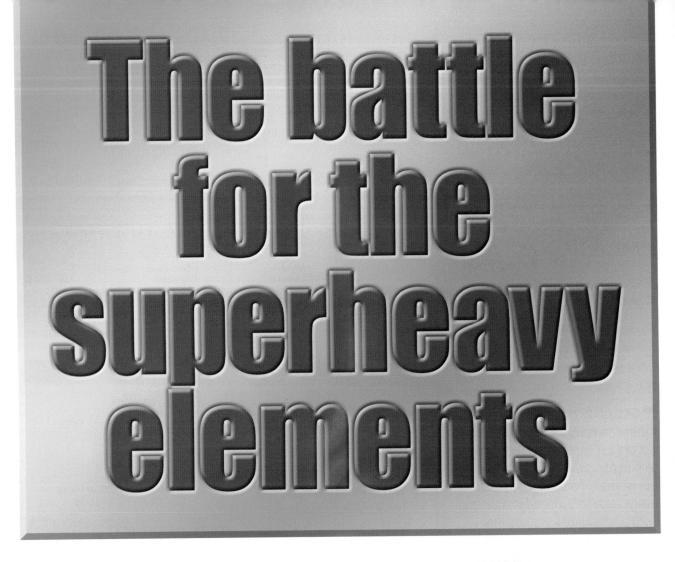

The battle for the superheavy elements

News that scientists at Lawrence Berkeley National Laboratory in the USA had created the heaviest element ever was beamed around the world in July 1999. Only two years later they were faced with retracting their claim when it seems that they had misinterpreted their results.

The periodic table of the elements started life when Dmitri Mendeleev had a dream where he saw the known elements laid out like cards in a game of patience. Many scientists were

				Ti 50	Zr 90	? 100
				V 51	Nb 94	Ta 182
				Cr 52	Mo 96	W 186
				Mn 55	Rh 104.4	Pt 197.4
				Fe 56	Ru 104.4	Ir 198
				Ni, Co 59	Pd 106.6	Os 199
H 1						
				Cu 63.4	Ag 108	Hg 200
	Be 9.4	Mg 24		Zn 65.2	Cd 112	
	B 11	Al 37.4		? 68	U 116	Au 197?
	C 12	Si 28		? 70	Sn 118	
	N 14	P 31		As 75	Sb 122	Bi 210?
	O 16	S 32		Se 79.4	Te 128?	
	F 19	Cl 35.5		Br 80	I 127	
Li 7		Na 23	K 39	Rb 85.4	Cs 133	Tl 204
			Ca 40	Sr 87.6	Ba 137	Pb 207
			? 45	Ce 92		
			Er? 56	La 94		
			Yt? 60	Di 95		
			In 75.6?	Th 118?		

« Mendeleev's imagination gave us the version of the periodic table we use today – though he had to leave gaps until some of the elements were discovered »

trying to work out the patterns in the known elements but only Mendeleev had the nerve to leave gaps where he felt that there was still an element to be discovered. The gaps spurred other scientists to look for elements that had the right combination of properties to fit the pattern.

Slowly all the gaps were filled and we have the periodic table of the elements that is today displayed in every laboratory in the country. Every element has a different number of protons from the one before, starting with hydrogen which has only one proton and going up to the heaviest elements with over 100 protons. The bottom row has grown slowly as scientists have created elements that do not exist in nature and only exist for a fraction of a second. This is where the Berkeley story starts.

> The nucleus of every atom is made of protons and neutrons (except for hydrogen which only has a single proton in it). Each element has a different number of protons. They all have different numbers of neutrons too – but the pattern is not so neat. Although the number of protons and the number of neutrons go up in step for a while, after that the neutrons start to outnumber the protons as the elements get heavier and heavier. The number of protons an element has is called its atomic number, while the total number of nucleons (protons and neutrons) is called its mass number.

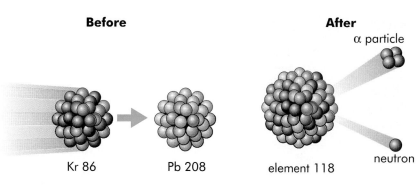

Before Kr 86 → Pb 208

After element 118

α particle

neutron

« Hitting lead with krypton was the recipe for making element 118. The evidence was the alpha particle that was emitted a fraction of a second later »

The race was on to create the heaviest element ever. Scientists in Dubna Laboratory in Russia had succeeded in making an element with 114 protons and 184 neutrons in early 1999. Just months later the Berkeley team announced that not only had it created an element with 116 protons but also that it had evidence of one with 118 protons. The discovery was so important that the team wrote up their work and had it published in one of the most prestigious scientific journals *Physical Review Letters.* Although both elements fell apart in less than a millisecond, scientists

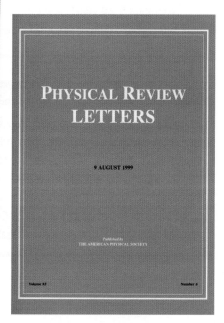

PHYSICAL REVIEW LETTERS

9 AUGUST 1999

Published by
THE AMERICAN PHYSICAL SOCIETY

Volume 83   Number 6

« The Berkeley team published their work in this important journal »

around the world were convinced and set about trying to replicate the experiment. It's not enough simply to tell the world you have succeeded, your work has to be repeated by independent teams if it is to be believed.

The experiment

To make element 118, the scientists at Berkeley had collided beams of krypton-86 ions with a lead-108 target. Krypton-86 has 36 protons and 50 neutrons while lead-208 has 82 protons and126 neutrons. The idea was to get the two nuclei to fuse together leaving a nucleus with 118 protons and 175 neutrons (the extra neutron was emitted during the reaction). Within a millisecond the new element, being radioactive, emitted an alpha particle. This left another new element with 116 protons and 173 neutrons.

Of course the team was only making a few atoms of this new element and it only lasted a millisecond, so it was impossible to do any tests on it to see what it was. The only way they knew they had made this new element was when they saw a stream of six high-energy alpha particles. This stream of alpha particles was, they said, the evidence that the new

Isotopes and ions

For some elements you can have isotopes. These atoms have the right number of protons but a different number of neutrons from 'normal'. Often these isotopes are radioactive, as they are heavier than normal atoms. To get back to a more 'stable' size they will often emit an alpha particle (two protons and two neutrons together).

Ions are atoms which have had some of their outer electrons removed so they are positively charged. They are often used in experiments because it is easy to fire them at things by attracting them towards a negative charge.

elements. After two years trying they had to admit failure. Although they very carefully copied every stage of the experiment, they did not see the telltale stream of six alpha particles. When the team at Berkeley heard this they went back and looked at their results again. After a lot of thinking, they decided to retract their claim and wrote a short statement for *Physical Review Letters*, which was published for all the scientific community to read in July 2001.

By Autumn 2002 the story had taken a more sinister turn. Lab Director Charles Shak had to admit that the data had been made up by one of the scientists who has now been fired. Even so, teams around the world are still looking for evidence for superheavy elements – and are being even more careful to check their results – and each others! ∎

element existed. For every 10^{21} (1 000 000 000 000 000 000 000) collisions between a krypton ion and a lead atom, only one atom of element 118 was made. Over the 11 days of the experiment they claimed to see three such streams of alpha particles.

As soon as teams in Japan and Germany read about the experiment they set out to repeat it, and to try to use the same method to make even heavier

Questions

1 What is the difference between an isotope and an ion?

2 The heaviest element ever made had 114 protons and 184 neutrons. What is its atomic number and its mass number?

3 What elements did the scientists at Berkeley use to try to make their heaviest element – number 118?

4 Very soon after it is made, element 118 should emit an alpha particle. Why does this happen?

5 What did the scientists at Berkeley do to make sure everyone knew the details of their experiment?

6 Why did other scientists around the world start to repeat the experiment as soon as they read about it?

7 No other team managed to get the same results as the Berkeley team. What happened next?

8 What do you think these scientists are doing now?

Extra activities

Scientists at universities are keen to publish as many papers in journals as they possibly can. In fact they often get promoted if they publish lots of papers, as this shows how clever they are and how hard they are working. Use the Internet to look at the website of a university near to you and look at the research section of the physics department. For each scientist it is possible to see a list of all the papers they have published. Look at a few pages and see how many papers scientists publish, typically, in a year.

Looking out of an aeroplane window you are almost dazzled by the bright white clouds as you pass over them. Even though clouds are made of water droplets and water is transparent, clouds are white. This is because each separate water droplet scatters all the colours of light that fall on it in every direction. Our eyes pick up all the colours of light and see the combination – which is white. (The sky is blue in a similar way. The gas particles of the air are just the right size to scatter the blue into our eyes.)

Rain, rain, go away

« The upper surface of clouds can be dazzling – but why are they white when water is transparent? »

But there's more to clouds than meets the eye. In the UK we see so many forms of cloud that we take them for granted and simply complain when they rain on us. Back in the 19th century, French artists would visit England just to practise painting clouds – even in France the variety of clouds is more limited!

But now it seems that polluted clouds in the northern hemisphere could be responsible for **reducing** global warming and **reducing** rainfall in some areas. To understand why, we have to go back to basics. How do clouds form and what makes them rain?

The air around us is full of water vapour, which is completely invisible to us. As convection currents make the warm air rise up

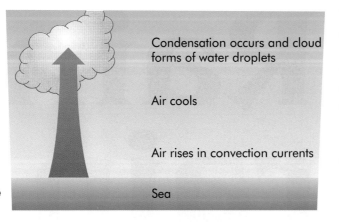

« Invisible water vapour rises on convection currents, cools down and condenses to form water droplets. Clouds are made of these water droplets »

Condensation occurs and cloud forms of water droplets

Air cools

Air rises in convection currents

Sea

it cools down. Eventually the water vapour reaches the higher regions of the atmosphere where it is so cold the water vapour condenses to form tiny water droplets. These water droplets are so small that they float in the air because the upthrust of the air is greater than the downward force of gravity on the droplets. This is what clouds are made of.

Layered clouds are called 'stratus' clouds. They form when different layers of air move past each other and can be several kilometres across.

« Layered clouds are 'stratus' clouds »

Simple vertical convection currents make vertical clouds – or cumulus clouds, such as the 'fluffy' clouds crossing the sky on a bright summer's day. Some cumulus clouds can be up to 16 kilometres

high, and several tonnes in weight with bright white tops and dark bases looking a bit like a cauliflower. These are cumulonimbus, which means 'rain-bearing' cumulus clouds.

« Cumulus clouds are the fluffy clouds we see on fine days »

The water droplets in a young cloud are too small to fall as rain. But slowly the droplets grow. First they attract surrounding water vapour and begin to swell. Then they begin to collide with each other and stick together making larger and larger water drops. When the drops reach about 0.2 millimetres in diameter they are heavy enough to fall through the cloud and the rainstorm begins.

But where does pollution come in? When the water vapour condenses it has to have a centre to condense around. It uses any particle of dirt it can find. Vapour trails behind jets speeding across a clear blue sky are evidence of this. At these high altitudes the temperature is cold enough for the water vapour to condense but if there are no dirt particles, the water remains as an invisible vapour. As soon as the exhaust fumes from the jet appear, the nearest water condenses onto the particles of dirt. You have probably seen the white trail of condensed water vapour left as a jet flies by.

In a polluted area there is so much dirt in the air that the water vapour condenses easily and forms lots of tiny water droplets. In normal 'clean' air there are fewer bits of dirt so the cloud forms with fewer but larger water droplets. Of course the droplets have to grow before they are heavy enough to fall as rain but it seems that the thousands of millions of water droplets in a polluted cloud are so tiny that they never get together to form large enough droplets. This is why polluted cloud can't rain very well.

« These cumulonimbus clouds are rain-bearing – they look like cauliflowers with dark bases »

« When the water droplets become big enough they can no longer float in the air so they fall as rain »

« The dirt in the jet's exhaust fumes acts as centres for the water droplets to form »

Questions

1 In the first line of the article we are told water is transparent. What does this mean?

2 If water is transparent, why is it surprising that clouds are white?

3 What explanation is given for the fact that clouds are white?

4 Why can we not see the water vapour that is all around us every day?

5 Why can we see the water vapour when it rises higher into the atmosphere?

6 Explain clearly how the dirt particles in the air help clouds to form.

7 Explain why polluted air is likely to make clouds that can't rain.

What has this to do with global warming? It seems that the tiny water droplets in polluted clouds reflect more of the Sun's radiation out into space. This means the amount of heating is less than if the clouds were 'clean'. This could be a reason why the southern hemisphere, which is less polluted, is warming up faster than the northern hemisphere.

So perhaps some types of pollution form rainless clouds and keep the Earth cooler. ■

Discussion

At the end of the article it claims that the southern hemisphere is warming up more quickly than the northern hemisphere. This seems to show that pollution in the form of dirt particles is saving us from the effects of global warming even though pollution in the form of greenhouse gases seems to be a cause of global warming. Do you think this shows that we should keep creating dirt particles and releasing them into the air, as this type of pollution causes reflecting clouds to form and reduces the effect of global warming?

Extra activities

Make a chart of the different types of cloud described in the article. For each one draw a sketch and list the most obvious features.

Time travel

BY JIM AL-KHALILI

« Jim Al-Khalili is a theoretical nuclear physicist and senior lecturer at the University of Surrey where he teaches courses on Einstein's relativity theory and quantum physics. He has appeared on TV and radio numerous times to discuss complex scientific ideas from the nature of time to the science of Star Wars. He has even explained how Dr Who's TARDIS might work. He has written *Black Holes, Wormholes and Time Machines* (Institute of Physics, 1999). When not being a scientist he follows Leeds United with his ten year-old son, David »

Time is a fascinating topic. Did we invent it or has it always been around? Does the future already exist? Is the past still happening? Can time speed up and slow down? Did it have a beginning? You may well think you have the answer to these questions.

Until Isaac Newton completed his work on the laws of motion in 1687, time was more philosophy than science. We have learnt a lot since then, and yet we are probably no closer to answering some of these questions.

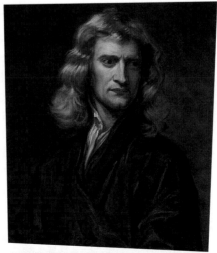

« Isaac Newton gave us some sensible ideas about forces and how things move »

Newton described how objects move when forces act on them. Since all movement and change needs the idea of time for it to make sense, time had to be included in the equations. Newton described time as something that exists entirely on its own outside of space and independent of everything. Sounds reasonable doesn't it?

For Newton, time flowed at a constant rate as though there were an imaginary cosmic clock that marked off the seconds, hours and years regardless of our personal sensation of time passing. We cannot make time speed up or slow down.

But was Newton right? Does a cosmic time really exist? Albert Einstein showed that it doesn't.

« Einstein completely rethought Newton's ideas about time »

Einstein's time

In 1905, Einstein discovered that time and space are related. This is his special theory of relativity. He had been struggling with the ideas leading up to it since he was a teenager. Today, popular accounts of special relativity will often tell you that Einstein's theory gave us the famous equation $E = mc^2$. This is true. However, special relativity goes much deeper than that. It started a revolution in physics. It showed how and why the old ideas of space and time had to be ditched and replaced with a new and unfamiliar set of ideas. The theory of relativity links time with the three dimensions of space into something called space-time. This is where the idea of time as the fourth dimension comes from. But even to this day, most of us have not been able to shake off the old Newtonian view of time.

In 1915, Einstein completed his general theory of relativity. This describes how gravity affects space-time and gives us many exciting predictions about the birth of the Universe in the 'big bang' and the existence of black holes.

Special relativity

But first let me say a little more about special relativity. Einstein showed that time runs more slowly for anyone travelling at speeds near to the speed of light (an impressive 300 000 kilometres per second). The closer to the speed

The closer to the speed of light that a clock moves, the slower it will tick.

of light that a clock moves, the slower it will tick. And before you dismiss this as 'just a theory', I should point out that time slowing down is easily demonstrated these days in particle accelerators. Particle accelerators are huge laboratories with underground tunnels several miles long that accelerate tiny sub-atomic particles to almost the speed of light. The most famous one is the CERN facility in Switzerland.

Let me give you a simple example. Imagine a sprinter who runs a hundred metres in exactly ten seconds, as measured by the reliable and highly accurate timekeeping of the judges. Time slows down very slightly for him while he is running so his watch would show a time of only 9.999 999 999 995 seconds. Of course, this is so close to ten seconds that we would never know the difference. The difference between the runner's and the judges' watches is just five 'picoseconds'. The reason time only slows down a tiny amount is because the athlete is moving so much slower than the speed of light.

Fast-Forward to the Future

This idea of time slowing down gives us a chance of time travel into the future. Here's how. If you were to travel in a rocket that could go at almost the speed of light, and you zipped around the Galaxy for, say, four years, then when you got home to Earth you would be in for a bit of a shock. If your on-board calendar says you left in January 2000 and returned in January 2004, then depending on your exact speed and how twisted your path was through the stars, you might find that, on Earth, the year is 2040 and everyone on Earth has aged 40 years! They would be equally shocked to see how young you still looked considering how long you had, according to them, been away.

So for you inside the rocket only four years have elapsed while Earth-bound clocks have counted off 40 years. This means that you have leapt 36 years into the future.

This effect has been checked and confirmed many times in very accurate experiments. Scientists have synchronised two highly accurate atomic clocks, then placed one of them on an aircraft and the other in a laboratory on Earth. After the aircraft had returned, the two clocks were checked again. It was found that they no longer agreed but were out by a fraction of a second. (Note that I am being picky here because it might be that the travelling clock actually comes back with more time elapsed. This is because we must also take into account the fact that gravity slows time down – a general relativity effect not discussed here. Therefore the stay-at-home clock runs more slowly by virtue of feeling a stronger gravitational field – closer to the Earth. The two effects act in opposite directions and which one wins depends on the altitude and speed of the aircraft! Sorry.) Even though the jet was travelling at 1000 kilometres per hour, the speed of light is still a million times faster. This is why

« Travelling through space at high speeds will make time flow more slowly for you than for the people you leave behind on Earth »

there is a very small difference between the two clocks. Nevertheless, that difference is real and the clocks are so accurate that we do not doubt their readings.

High-speed motion really does allow time travel to the future.

What's done is done

It turns out that time travel to the past is much more difficult. To many people, it might come as a surprise that travelling forward in time is easier than travelling back in time. If anything, you might think that the idea of travelling into the future is more ridiculous. At least the past is out there in some sense – it has happened. The future, on the other hand, has not yet happened. How can we visit a time that has not happened yet? But of course time travel to the future by high-speed motion does not need the future to be already 'out there' waiting for us. Instead, we have to move out of our normal time frame

and into one in which time moves more slowly. While we are in this state, time outside is ticking by more quickly and the future is unfolding at high speed. When we rejoin our original time frame we will have reached the future more quickly than everyone else will.

On the other hand, there are many mind-boggling examples of how ridiculous things would be if time travel to the past were possible. For example, what if you were to go back in time, to last year say, and kill your younger self. What happens then? Do you simply stop existing as the 'younger you' slumps to the ground? And if you died last year, who killed you? I know this is a bit morbid, but it is a well-known paradox. Think about it. It seems you cannot kill yourself because you must survive the assassination attempt to become the assassin. The thing you have to remember about time travel to the past, if it is possible, is that you are allowed to meddle with history as long as things turn out the way they do. You cannot *change* the past.

Back to the past

In principle, there would be two ways of going back to the past. One is by going *backwards* through time, during which the hands on your watch would be moving round anticlockwise. This would require faster-than-light

> **...this kind of time travel into the past is, theoretically, possible.**

speeds that are not possible for us, and so is not the sort of time travel I am discussing here. The other way is you travel forward in time (your watch runs forwards) but you move along a warped path through space-time that takes you back to your past (like looping the loop on a roller coaster). Such a loop is known in physics as a 'closed time-like curve'. What may come as a surprise to you is that it has been known for half a century that Einstein's equations of general relativity allow these closed time-like curves to exist. Kurt Gödel, an American mathematician, showed in 1949 that this kind of time travel into the past is, theoretically, possible.

So what is all the fuss about? Time travel to the future has been done and time travel to the past, while difficult, is not yet ruled out by theory. What are we waiting for? Why haven't we built a time machine yet? The problem is that, apart from it being exceedingly

« Is there a naturally-occurring time machine somewhere in the universe, a closed time-like curve? »

difficult to create closed time-like curves in space-time, we do not really understand them anyway. As things stand, at the beginning of the 21st century, general relativity tells us that we cannot rule out time travel, but many physicists are hoping that a better understanding of the mathematics will eventually lead to the conclusion that time loops are forbidden.

At the moment, we cannot completely rule out the possibility that a naturally-occurring time machine exists somewhere in the Universe. It is theoretically possible for space-time to be so warped due to a very strong gravitational field that under certain special conditions a time loop is created. If we stumble across such a thing, known as a wormhole, during future space travel it may provide

us with a permanent link to the past.

Where are all the time travellers?

For now, the only way we can prove that time loops cannot exist is to ask where all the time travellers from the future are? If future generations ever succeed in building a time machine then surely there will be many who would wish to visit our time and we should see these visitors among us today. So just to keep the debate alive I will list five possible reasons why we should not expect to see any time travellers:

1   Time travel to the past may be forbidden by some as yet undiscovered laws of physics. Physicists hope to discover a new theory that goes beyond

general relativity and which explains why time loops are forbidden. We already have two possible candidates for such a theory, know as 'superstring theory' and 'membrane theory'. But neither is properly understood yet.

2 If naturally-occurring time machines, such as wormholes, do not exist then the only way to travel back in time would be to build one ourselves. But it turns out that this would only take us as far back as the moment it was switched on (because of the way it would hook up space and time). So we do not see time travellers from the future because time machines have not been invented yet.

3 Naturally-occurring time machines do exist and people do use them to travel back to the 21st century. But it turns out that our Universe is just one of an infinite number of parallel universes. In that case, time travel to the past would slide the traveller into a parallel world. There are so many of these that our Universe is just not one of the lucky few that have been visited.

If you are not convinced by these ideas then I might interest you in a couple of more mundane possibilities:

4 Expecting to see time travellers among us assumes that they would want to visit this century. Maybe for them there will be much nicer and safer periods to visit.

5 Time travellers from the future are among us but keep a low profile!

If I were a betting man I would say that time travel to the past will soon be shown to be impossible even in theory. Getting to the future, on the other hand, just requires us to build a fast enough rocket. Beware though that if you reach the future, there is no coming back. ∎

Questions

1 What is the difference between Newton's idea of time and Einstein's idea of time?

2 Describe what might happen if you went on a long journey in a space rocket, according to the article.

3 Does it seem that travelling forward in time is easier or harder than travelling backwards in time? Why is this?

4 There's one real problem with the idea of travelling to the past – you could kill your 'younger self'. Why is this a problem?

Discussion

At the end of the article there are several ideas put forward which explain why we haven't seen time travellers from the future. Which one do you find most convincing? Explain why you prefer this one to the others.

Is nuclear power the only way to save the environment?

Governments are in a dilemma. Should they adopt an energy policy that is popular with the voting public at the moment or should they consider the long-term options? Are they prepared to put up taxes to pay for the research and development that is needed to solve the energy crisis?

Ask most people and they will reply that they would like all our electricity to be generated from renewable sources. But we now consume so much energy that no single source can satisfy our needs. It will take a long time to develop the technology and to build all the power stations, and our needs are urgent. In the mean time should nuclear power play any part in future energy generation? Where do you think the government should spend your money?

Here we list the pros and cons of nuclear energy generation compared with fossil fuels and renewable sources.

Nuclear power

Should we continue to build nuclear power stations? Should we close down all the nuclear power stations? Is it worth investing money in finding better ways of disposing of nuclear waste?

- A nuclear power station has no harmful effects on the environment – it produces no dirt, greenhouse gases or other polluting chemicals.

- The nuclear waste is a long-term hazard to the environment, which is expensive to deal with.

- Nuclear power already produces 50% of the energy needs of Western Europe (80% in France).

- The amount of money spent by the government on nuclear power in the last five years is about 100 times as much as has been given to develop renewable energy.

- By 2010, the UK will have stockpiled about 100 tonnes of plutonium from reprocessing spent nuclear fuel – about two-thirds of the world's total.

- Some of the waste products are a serious risk to the proliferation of nuclear weapons.

- Using nuclear power stations has reduced the amount of pollution in the UK – already the amount of carbon dioxide has been reduced by 3000 million tonnes. As present nuclear power stations are decommissioned, the UK will find it impossible to meet its target for reducing its carbon dioxide emissions.

- The technology for treating nuclear waste is well known – it can be fused into insoluble ceramic blocks and stored in geologically stable underground bunkers.

- The latest technology is finding ways of taking the high level nuclear waste from power stations and 'transmuting' it into material which is still radioactive but which has a much shorter half-life – a few years instead of several thousand years. It will take a lot more money for research into this before it is perfected, but it might be worth it.

- Keeping nuclear power stations and the stored nuclear waste safe requires high technology. This can be very costly.

Fossil Fuels

Should we continue to build coal fired power stations? Should we continue to burn oil? Should we build more gas-fired power stations. Should we stop using fossil fuels to help reduce global warming?

- Known oil reserves are fast running out – only 100–200 years worth. We really need them to produce medicines and polymers. Burning oil in power stations and in cars is just wasteful.

- Recent estimates show that there are far more fossil fuels still buried than we previously thought – perhaps up to 450 years of natural gas if we keep using it at present day rates. Scientists also think that there are huge amounts of natural gas hidden under the permafrosts in Siberia and under the ocean floor. This would cost a lot more to extract than the reserves we are using at the moment, but this might be money well spent.

- Known coal reserves will last about 200–250 years but it is possible that there are undiscovered areas with enough coal to last 1500 years. It will be much more expensive

More people have died in the coal mining industry than in any nuclear accident.

to extract than our present reserves.

- A coal fired power station pumps out 11 million tonnes of the greenhouse gas carbon dioxide each year. This adds to global warming. The same coal fired power station also pumps out nearly 600 000 tonnes of other polluting materials including up to one tonne of radioactive uranium. The gases it pumps out are bad for out health and, in particular, cause problems for people with asthma.

- Sulphur dioxide and other impurities produced when burning fossil fuels cause acid rain which destroys rivers and forests.

- More people have died in the coal mining industry than in any nuclear accident. Coal mining is still a very dangerous occupation in countries like China and India.

- In the short term, fossil fuels seem cheap but you have to dial in the costs of cleaning up the pollution and the effects of climate change. Already some species have become extinct because of climate change that may be related to global warming.

- Gas-fired power stations emit only half as much carbon dioxide as coal-fired power stations but they do give out methane which is also a very powerful greenhouse gas.

Renewables

- Hydro-electric power uses up valuable land and destroys habitats when a valley is flooded. Because of the limits of geography, it is unlikely that hydro-electric power can provide more than 8% of our energy needs in the UK.

- Wind and solar power are unreliable and take up large areas of land or coastline.

- Tidal power is intermittent and the barrages are a hazard to shipping.

- Wind and solar power are expensive and dangerous. Already five times as many people have died during solar and wind power energy production than during energy production from nuclear power.

- Wind and solar power only provide about 0.15% of the world's energy requirements – and this requires large areas of land for wind farms or solar cells. There is no real hope that these types of power can provide all our energy needs.

- In theory the whole of the world's energy needs could be met by covering 1% of the land now used for crops or pasture with solar cells.

- Solar technologies are more economical in the hotter areas where the developing nations are located.

Wind and solar power only provide about 0.15% of the world's energy requirements

- Although wind turbines are often accused of being unattractive, more are now being installed offshore.

- There is some concern that large numbers of wind turbines will affect wind patterns and, therefore, weather patterns.

- Hydrogen fuel cells powered from hydrogen produced from natural gas are looking promising – they can be used to generate electricity and provide heat – and even to drive cars with almost zero pollution. Making hydrogen from water by electrolysis is also a good way of storing the energy produced from solar and wind power. More research is still needed on this.

- To keep carbon dioxide emission levels the same as they are at the moment we would need to replace one fossil fuel power station per week for the next 40 years. This would require 500 m^2 land for 4000 wind turbines each week, or covering 10 km^2 desert with solar panels per week, or building a tidal barrage across a river each week.

- To build a wind farm to generate the same power as a single conventional power station we would need to put up a wind turbine every day for the next 10 years – that's a lot of wind turbines and they need a lot of space.

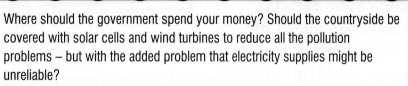

Discussion

Where should the government spend your money? Should the countryside be covered with solar cells and wind turbines to reduce all the pollution problems – but with the added problem that electricity supplies might be unreliable?

In the meantime:

- Should nuclear power stations replace existing fossil fuel stations as we try to reduce pollution and global warming – but with the added cost of finding better ways to deal with the nuclear waste?

- Should fossil fuel stations replace existing nuclear stations as we make them more efficient and find further reserves – but with the added problem of pollution and the extra cost of extracting the more difficult reserves?

X-rays

promises and threats

When X-rays were first discovered they became an overnight success. Everyone wanted some of the action. People bought 'sleep-enhancing pillows' with pieces of radioactive material in them. They invested in plutonium pots – water storage vessels with radioactive materials in – as radiation dosed water was seen as 'beneficial to health' and ladies would invest in whalebone corsets containing pieces of radioactive material as these would 'give relief from back pain'. X-rays were soon used to check that children's shoes fitted correctly. Now we are more careful about exposing ourselves to X-rays.

« Victorian ladies bought corsets with radioactive materials in them because they believed it helped their backache »

Marie Curie and her daughter Irene were the first people to think of using X-rays for medical purposes. During the First World War, they persuaded doctors treating soldiers injured in battle that X-rays could give a picture of broken bones. Soldiers recovered much more quickly when doctors knew exactly which bit of the limb was broken and fewer soldiers had to have their limbs amputated.

Now we are completely used to the idea of using X-rays to see broken bones but we also know that we have to be careful how we use X-rays.

Paul Sellin is a physicist working at the University of Surrey whose work will make sure we receive a lower X-ray dose every time we need an X-ray. In this interview he talks about his work.

X-rays are high-energy (high frequency) electromagnetic waves. They are part of the electromagnetic spectrum which includes gamma rays, X-rays, ultra-violet rays, visible light, infra-red rays, microwaves and radio waves (in order of increasing wavelength). All electromagnetic waves have one thing in common – they can travel at the same speed (300 000 000 m/s) through a vacuum.

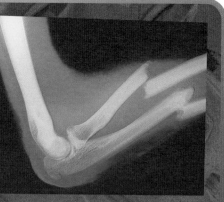

« The X-ray image shows broken bones clearly »

X-rays and gamma rays are different from the rest of the spectrum – they can penetrate most substances, including human flesh. When a doctor takes a conventional X-ray of your broken arm, the X-rays are fired at your arm while a photographic film lies underneath. The X-rays that go through your flesh hit the film while those that cannot go through your bones cast a shadow.

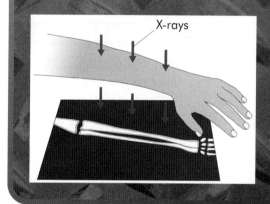

« X-ray images work because X-rays cannot go through your bones and so a shadow is cast on the X-ray film »

Q. Why is it important to make sure we receive lower doses of X-rays if we have an X-ray taken at a hospital or at the dentist?

Paul: We have known for a long time that X-rays damage tissue. In fact doctors use this fact when they use very high energy X-rays to kill tumours in cancer patients. But for the rest of us it's simply sensible to keep our X-ray dose as low as possible.

Q. Tell me how your work helps with this.

Paul: I'm working on digital X-ray cameras. We know that digital cameras can take normal photos in lower light conditions than the old-fashioned film cameras. My X-ray cameras work in the same way. The camera can take a digital X-ray image of a broken limb but it takes fewer X-rays to do it than the old fashioned film, so it is better for the patient.

Q. Does this mean we should be worried when we go for an X-ray?

Paul: Not at all. In fact on average our X-ray dose from medical sources is only 10% of our total annual radiation dose. That's about the same as the dose we get naturally from cosmic rays from outer space. Well over half the radiation you receive annually comes from background radiation – the rocks in the ground etc. and we've evolved to live happily with that.

Q. So how are your X-ray detectors different from the ones we've seen in hospitals?

Paul: My X-ray cameras can be quite tiny. For example, if you have had a dental X-ray you will probably have held a piece of X-ray film between your teeth while the enormous X-ray source is aimed at your jaw. We will soon be able to use miniature digital X-ray cameras that you hold in your mouth. This will give an instant picture on a screen that the dentist can look at so you won't have to wait for the film to be developed. You can even take a copy home on a disc!

We will also be able to take X-ray movies. This is extremely useful, for example, when a surgeon has to insert a catheter into an artery and steer it into your brain to seal off bleeding. The X-ray movie can watch the catheter as it moves into your brain and

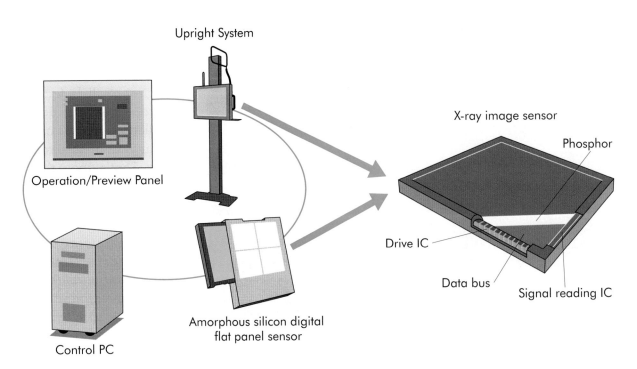

Upright System

Operation/Preview Panel

Control PC

Amorphous silicon digital
flat panel sensor

X-ray image sensor

Phosphor

Drive IC

Data bus

Signal reading IC

« Mini digital X-ray cameras will make going to the dentist a very different experience »

« Paul Sellin
from the
University of
Surrey is
working on X-ray
machines that
give us lower
doses of X-rays
when we have
an X-ray taken »

the surgeon can be quite
sure it is exactly in the right
place before he/she presses
the button and puts a dob of
glue to seal the haemorrhage.
Medical X-rays may have
been around for a very long
time, but scientists are still
working to make them safer
all the time. ■

MOBILE PHONES

what's the truth?

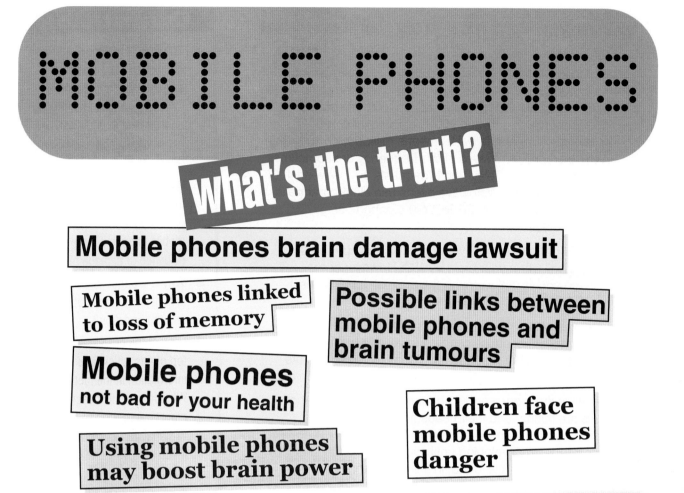

Mobile phones brain damage lawsuit

Mobile phones linked to loss of memory

Possible links between mobile phones and brain tumours

Mobile phones not bad for your health

Children face mobile phones danger

Using mobile phones may boost brain power

Mobile Phones Warning Creates Confusion

Friday 12th May 2000

An official government report has added to the confusion about the possible health risks and benefits that are linked with using mobile phones. The report, published yesterday, found that there was no evidence that mobile phones caused damage to health. However the report also concluded that there was no evidence that mobile phones did not damage health.

Research had shown that although the microwaves generated by mobile phones are not strong enough to heat up brain tissue, they may switch on genes that would normally be switched on by stress. This may lead to what it called a 'subtle biological effect'.

The head of the enquiry, Sir William Stewart, is quoted as saying 'I don't want you to go away with the impression that mobile phones are responsible for ill effects all over the place.' But he went on to add that children should be discouraged from using mobile phones regularly and should only use them for emergencies.

The mobile phones industry is understandably concerned by this recommendation as the report failed to define what it meant by children. A spokesman said, 'If you're talking about teenagers, the effect on business could be worrying. Young people account for 25% of the mobile phone market.'

The report also said there was no evidence that mobile phone masts were a danger to residents or children in schools. However the report then went on to recommend stricter planning restrictions on where masts may be sited because worrying about possible health risks could be making people ill – a so-called 'indirect health risk'.

The main group at risk from using mobile phones, however, is car drivers. Talking on a phone is very distracting and has already caused a large number of accidents!

FACT BOX

- Mobile phones are low power radio devices that transmit and receive electromagnetic radiation. The radio waves they use are quite high frequency compared with the radio waves we use for radio and television stations. Mobile phones work on a frequency of between 900 megahertz and 1800 megahertz. (Megahertz (MHz) means million hertz or million waves per second.) Waves of this frequency are sometimes called microwaves. Television broadcasts are between 400 MHz and 860 MHz. Microwave ovens use electromagnetic waves at a frequency of 30 GHz (30 gigahertz or 30 000 000 000 Hz).

- A mobile phone can heat your brain but only by 0.1°C. Jogging will warm your brain by 1°C. However some research shows that warming the brain slightly makes it respond more quickly to problems.

- Radio waves do not carry enough energy to affect the DNA in cells so cannot cause cancer. However it has been suggested that the warming effect may increase the rate cancer develops, though more research is needed on this.

- Scientists are more worried about children because their skulls are thinner and their heads are smaller so the microwave radiation will go deeper into the brain. A child's brain keeps on developing until mid teens so may be more easily damaged if it is found, in the future, that there are health risks.

- Research has shown that microwaves can produce stress in animals.

- The SAR (specific absorption rate) for any mobile phone tells you the amount of radio wave energy your body receives from the phone. All mobile phones have to be below the SAR limit for human health.

- Research has shown that hands-free sets increase the levels of radiation entering the user's head.

Questions

1 The official government report concluded there was no evidence that mobile phones caused damage to health and no evidence that they did not cause damage to health. Why do you think it concluded this?

2 Why does the report conclude that children should be discouraged from using mobile phones if there is no evidence of damage to health?

3 Why is the mobile phone industry concerned about this recommendation?

4 Look at the headlines at the top of this article and at the information in the facts box. Why do you think each reporter wrote his or her piece with that particular headline? If you read only one of these articles do you think you would get a realistic view of the risk of mobile phones?

5 'Absence of evidence' is not the same as 'evidence of absence!' Explain how these two phrases are different. Why does this make it very difficult for scientists to be 100% certain of their findings?

Extra activities

Look at the information in the box and decide whether the conclusions of the report are fair and what evidence you used to make your conclusion.

a) Is it fair to say that we can keep on using mobile phones without worrying about health risks? Evidence?

b) Is it fair to say that children should be discouraged from using mobile phones? Evidence?

c) Is it fair to conclude that the people most at risk when using mobile phones are drivers? Evidence?

d) Is it fair to conclude that mobile phone masts should not be situated near to schools? Evidence?

ISIS

THE BIGGEST IN THE WORLD!

Deep in the Oxfordshire countryside is a large building. Every morning hundreds of people turn up for work and find themselves in pleasant offices with carpeted floors and modern computers on their desks. They may take a break in the airy coffee lounge, chat to friends over lunch in the restaurant, or they may take a stroll in the grounds.

《 The Rutherford Appleton laboratories in Oxfordshire 》

But this is no ordinary place of work. Look a little further and you will find the largest source of neutrons in the world. It is the size of several football pitches and consumes the same amount of electricity as a small town. This is ISIS at the Rutherford Appleton Laboratory (RAL). The people working here are scientists and they are doing everything from biotechnology to engineering, from earth science to materials science, from pharmacology to physics.

Probing ...

ISIS does what Rutherford's experiment did (see blue box) – it probes matter to find out what's in there. The scientists are looking at why soaps do what they do, or how water molecules arrange themselves and why they won't mix with oil. They are interested in how the magnetic materials in computer hard disks work, how drug molecules function, what happens when a huge engineering component is put under stress or what happens to materials under extreme conditions like those at the centre of the Earth. They are producing the next generation of superconductors and trying to find out how to make batteries powerful enough to drive cars.

Rutherford fired alpha particles at gold foil. At ISIS scientists fire neutrons at their chosen target. Neutrons are one of the two particles in the nucleus of the atom. They have no charge but they are 2000 times as heavy as an electron

ERNEST RUTHERFORD

Ernest Rutherford was a student of J.J. Thomson in Cambridge in the 1890s. J.J. was famous for discovering the electron – the first subatomic particle to be discovered. Ernest first started working on radioactivity, where one atom changes to another by emitting an alpha or a beta particle. He later moved to Manchester University where

he set his students, Hans Geiger and Ernest Marsden, the job of firing alpha particles at gold foil. They had to sit in the dark for hours watching for flashes of light that showed where the alpha particles landed after they had hit the gold foil. The results were a shock. Some of the alpha particles bounced straight back from where they came. Others were deflected at odd angles as they went through. Up to this point everyone thought that atoms were simply a mixture of positive and negative particles in a ball – they called it the 'plum pudding' atom. 'This was as if you fired a gun at a piece of paper and a bullet came back and hit you in the face,' Rutherford said later.

The only conclusion they could come to was that most of the atom was empty space and that all the mass (and positive charge) was concentrated in a tiny space in the middle. They called it the nucleus. When an alpha particle missed the nucleus it went straight through the foil very easily. If it went close it would be repelled by the positive charge on the nucleus because the alpha particle is positively charged. If it interacted with the nucleus head on it would bounce straight back.

Rutherford's version of the atom was quickly accepted because he could predict which way alpha particles would go if you used different metal foils with different size (and charge) nuclei. This showed his theory didn't just work for gold.

» Ernest Rutherford supervised Hans Geiger and Ernest Marsden as their experiment disproved what everyone thought about the atoms at the time »

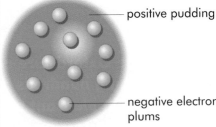

positive pudding

negative electron plums

» Before Rutherford did his experiment, everyone thought the atom was simply a mix of positively and negatively charged particles »

» Rutherford had to use his imagination to work out what was inside the atom. The idea of the nuclear atom that was mostly empty space took some imagination! »

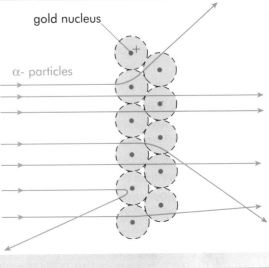

gold nucleus

α- particles

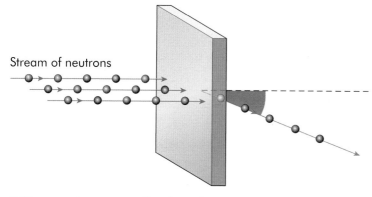

Stream of neutrons

« The neutrons are fired at the target and come out the other side. The direction in which they go tells us how the atoms are arranged »

(the same mass as a proton). Like Rutherford, the scientists here detect the neutrons as they come out of the target material – but this is now all done automatically, there's no sitting in the dark for hours. Everything is monitored by computer so you can leave the experiment running and go for a coffee if you want! The computer keeps a check on which direction the neutrons go as they come out of the material. From this pattern the scientists can tell how the atoms in the material are arranged.

Going exotic ...

ISIS doesn't only produce neutrons. It also produces exotic particles called muons which only live for two millionths of a second – but that's still long enough for computers to detect and monitor what they are doing. Muons are just one of a huge collection of particles that we are only just finding out about. A whole team of scientists at RAL spend their time probing not just the inside of atoms but also what's inside the nucleus. These are the particle physicists. And although they are looking at the tiniest things in the universe, they are taking part in the biggest experiment in the world!

The missing link

The team of particle physicists at RAL, led by Ken Peach, is helping to look for the missing link – the final piece of the puzzle that will

help to answer questions like: What exactly happened at the moment of the Big Bang? Why is there so much more matter than antimatter in the universe? Why do things have mass?

Some people believe there are particles called gravitons that carry the force of gravity – but no one has ever seen one. Others think that there is a particle called the Higgs boson, which causes things to have mass (when they interact with it). Experiments done by people in Ken's team working at CERN in Switzerland gave tantalising glimpses of what might have been a Higgs boson. But it was too little too late.

The standard model

Scientists now believe that protons and neutrons are not the end of the story. Inside a proton are three smaller particles called quarks – two 'up' quarks and one 'down' quark. Neutrons are a bit different. They are made of two 'down' quarks and one 'up' quark.

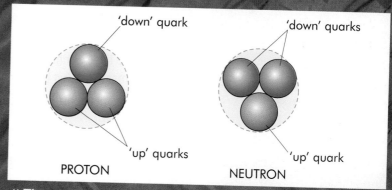

'down' quark   'down' quarks

'up' quarks   'up' quark

PROTON   NEUTRON

« The proton and neutron are made of three quarks. Changing a 'down' quark into an 'up' quark turns the neutron into a proton and results in a beta particle being emitted from the nucleus »

We know that when an unstable nucleus emits a beta particle one of its neutrons turns into a proton and the beta particle is the left-over negative charge – an electron. The standard model can give us more detail. If we look at the quarks that make up a neutron we can see that turning a down quark into an up quark makes the neutron into a proton. This is what we believe happens in beta decay.

Bill Murray, one of the team, takes up the story 'The excitement was amazing. The machine was in its last months of operation and we argued every way we could that it should be kept running so we could know whether or not we had found something. A five-week extension was granted but the new data were not sufficiently convincing. The apparatus (LEP – large electron collider) was closed in November 2000. The tunnel was needed to install the new LHC (large hadron collider) machine. No other machine can give us such pure results so we won't know for years now whether we were the first people to see a Higgs boson. But LHC is designed to find the Higgs particle, and will do it, if the American Tevatron does not do it first.'

And just to show scientists can have fun, RAL recently took up the challenge to create the world's smallest advert for the launch of the *Guinness Book of Records'* website. The result was an advert so small it could fit on a bee's knee with room to spare.

« The world's smallest advert made at RAL fits on a bee's knee »

EDWARD APPLETON

The Rutherford Appleton Laboratory is named after Ernest Rutherford and Edward Appleton.

Edward Appleton (1892–1965) was famous for working out that radio waves could be reflected off a layer of the atmosphere called the ionosphere. The ionosphere layer is between 60 km and 1000 km above the Earth. It has this name because it contains a large concentration of free electrons (negative ions). This is caused by ionizing radiation going through the ionosphere from space. Alpha or beta particles are called ionizing radiation because they can remove an electron from an atom when they collide with it and therefore make it into an ion. The part of the ionosphere that reflects radio waves is between 150 km and 1000 km above the Earth and has the highest concentration of ions. This layer is now called the Appleton Layer after Edward.

Questions

1 Draw diagrams of the plum pudding atom and Rutherford's nuclear atom. Point out the differences between them.

2 Why did Rutherford have to use his imagination when his experiment didn't give the results he expected?

3 Rutherford's idea of the atom was quickly accepted by his colleagues. Why was this?

4 Why are the experiments scientists do at ISIS similar to Rutherford's experiment? In what ways are they different?

5 ISIS uses neutrons. What are the differences between a neutron and a proton?

6 Scientists now believe that neutrons and protons are made of other particles. What are these smaller particles?

7 The particle physicists are still looking for evidence of particles that have never been seen. Why have they been frustrated in their work looking for the Higgs boson particle?

Extra activities

1 The Rutherford Appleton Laboratories do far more than this article can tell you. Look at their web site and find out what other facilities they have on www.clrc.ac.uk.

2 You might find it interesting to look at the on-line science club on www.sci-art.clrc.ac.uk.

A day in the life ...

People always think of universities as being a bit like large schools. In fact lecturers spend less than half their time teaching and they certainly don't get the same holidays as the students. So what do they get up to and how different is being a student at university compared with being at school? Here we follow some people from the Physics Department at Royal Holloway College, University of London to see what they got up to in a typical day.

Malte Grosche is from Germany but came to the UK when he was 18. He has recently become a lecturer in the department but he has been doing research for several years.

Q. What do you like about being a lecturer?

Malte: I have to spend quite a lot of time preparing my lectures and it's good to have the time to read and think about what I'm teaching. Now I can see how I would like to have been taught. I particularly enjoy it when students ask questions during lectures. They sometimes have trouble with some of the ideas and I have to change the way I explain things.

Q. What else do you have to do?

Malte: Part of the time I supervise older students who are working for their doctorate (PhD). Richard Burrell is one of my students. He studied here for his physics degree, then decided to stay on.

Q. Richard, why did you decide to stay on for a PhD?

Richard: I did some experiments on low-temperature physics in my second and third year and got hooked. I just wanted to learn more. I could have gone somewhere else but I'd enjoyed my time here so I decided to stay.

Q. Are there many students doing PhDs?

Richard: I think there are about 25 postgraduates. Eight or nine are working in low-temperature physics.

Q. How has it been so far?

Richard: I've only been at this for five months, so I'm still spending a lot of time reading papers in journals. Everyone who does a successful experiment will want to write it up and get it published in a journal. I have to read what everyone else has done and understand what they think the explanations are. Of course they might be wrong, but that's why the rest of us try to repeat their experiments, to check.

Q. What else have you had to do?

Richard: I'm sorting out the apparatus and learning how it works. It's a sort of 'fridge' 2 m tall and 50 cm in diameter and I need to get it to reach temperatures of about 300mK (0.3K, or almost −273°C).

Q. Do you spend all your time in the lab?

Richard: No. In fact I'm due to go to a conference in April in Brighton. There will be scientists from all over the world including several Nobel Prize winners. Conferences are where we hear about the latest findings and get to talk to everyone else who works in low temperature physics. It's nice to meet people when you've seen their names on papers in journals.

Q. Malte, you are supervising Richard's work. What is your own area of expertise?

Malte: The way electrons behave in metals at very low temperatures – phenomena such as superconductivity and magnetism. I use high pressure to change the properties of metals. For example, at very low temperatures we can remove magnetism from a metal by applying pressure. But you have to go to as much as 100 000 atmospheres.

Q. And have you found out anything unexpected?

Malte: Yes, I was part of a team in 1994/95 that discovered the first of a series of materials in which magnetism is linked very closely to superconductivity. We presented our findings at a conference in Warwick, then at one in Goa in India. People were excited but doubtful. Most people believed that you couldn't have magnetism and superconductivity at the same time. We had shown that superconductivity might actually be caused by magnetism. It seems that, at very low temperatures, you get little 'bubbles' of magnetism as electrons pass through the substance. If two electrons see each other's bubble of magnetism, they can interact. This might explain how they form the pairs that give us superconductivity. If this mechanism could help us devise room temperature superconductors, it would have an enormous technological potential and may lead to a Nobel Prize.

Q. So did you publish this in a journal?

Malte: We sent it to a journal but it has to be read by other scientists so that they can be sure it makes sense before the journal agrees to print it. People took a long time to be convinced so it took a long time for the paper to appear in print. In the mean time others had done similar things and got their papers published. It was very frustrating at the time, but we did get our priority established clearly in the end.

Robert Bennett, Helen Cheesworth and Robin Emmerson are students at Royal Holloway. What do they think of studying physics here?

Robert: I'm in the first year. Some things here are just like school, others are very different. It's a small department so you only get 30 people in a lecture. There are lots of places where there are 100 or even 200 people in a lecture. I get 15 lectures in a week. Some of the topics are the same as A-level, others like quantum mechanics are completely different. Then you get problem sheets for each course.

Helen: In the second year it's not that much different though you get to learn more about what's at the cutting edge of physics. All the space science and particle physics stuff is fascinating. You also begin to see how all areas of physics complement each other and link together.

Robert: Then you get a whole day in the labs each week. That's totally different from school. The experiments here can last six hours. You're really learning how professional physicists work rather than just doing an experiment.

Helen: I'm particularly looking forward to beginning my third year project. That's an experiment that lasts several weeks and counts as a whole course unit. I hope to do my project on space science – real hands-on use of a telescope. What you see is so beautiful and will make writing up so much more interesting!

Robin: I love doing the practical projects with lots of hands-on stuff. For my third year project I'm writing software for constructing astronomical images from the telescopes on the roof here. I hope to work in computing when I leave. I've already worked for the computer centre at the university over the summer vacations so I've got a good idea what it's about.

Helen: I actually chose physics because you can go into any career with a physics qualification. But, I'm really a dancer first and a physicist second. I was in a show over the summer, touring the country and I'm aiming to qualify for the World Irish Dance Championships. In my dance troupe most of us are scientists. That's quite unusual.

Robin: I didn't come to university straight away. I joined the army at 17 as an electronics engineer. I am dyslexic but I didn't find out until recently. It explains why I didn't do very well at school. Now I use word processors as they make all the difference. I have one I can talk to rather than typing. Since I came to university I've realized that the lecturers are very good, they treat you like human beings, and they're always willing to help you. They're a lot less intimidating than I thought they'd be.

Robert: It's good in the tutorials too. A group of four of us gets together with our tutor, Dr Tania McMahon, for an hour each week. It's a chance to sit round and talk about anything we want. It might be general physics or it might be problems with the work – anything really.

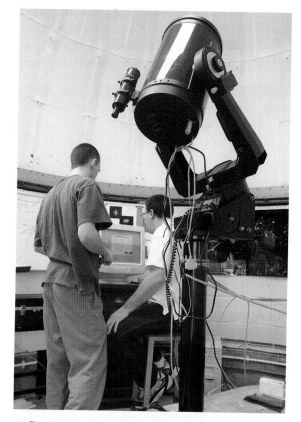

« Students analyse data from the computer-controlled Schmidt-Cassegrain telescope »

Robert had just come out of a maths lecture with Professor Moreton Moore. Professor Moore is famous for his knowledge of how diamonds form. But what has that to do with physics?

Moreton: I use X-rays to create images of diamonds to see any defects in them. Doing this tells us how the diamonds have grown. It is possible to grow diamonds and these experiments show us how to grow more perfect ones. However it's still cheaper to dig gem-quality diamonds out of the ground! Of course you can't find naturally-occurring diamonds in the UK, as they have to be brought to the surface by volcanoes. If there are any under the UK, they are too deep to get at. One of the things I have shown is that diamonds can dissolve in the molten rock of the Earth – and this explains why they occur in a range of shapes.

Q. So why are you lecturing in maths if you are a diamond expert?

Moreton: I did a degree in maths so I enjoy teaching maths, especially geometry. This morning I was using a kitchen strainer and a large potato because I was talking about the mathematics of surfaces. I like to use interesting demonstrations in my lectures.

Questions

1 How do science journals make sure that they only publish high-quality papers?

2 Why do other scientists try to repeat experiments they have read about in journals?

3 Malte found it difficult to get his ideas about magnetism and superconductivity published. Why was this?

4 At the moment there are some people who believe that magnetism is not related to superconductivity, others believe they are related. How will they resolve this disagreement?

5 Moreton has travelled all over the world to conferences and Richard is soon to go to his first conference. Why do scientists get invited to all these conferences?

WEBSITES

www.ph.rhul.ac.uk

« Royal Holloway's 30 cm computer-controlled Schmidt-Cassegrain telescope »

Holey Earth

A group of Spanish scientists has come up with a crazy idea. They claim that it should be possible to surround a city with huge holes and shield it from earthquakes.

The Spanish team has already shown that they can block light by drilling a network of fine holes through a substance. The holes scatter the light and the substance becomes opaque. They also know it is possible to block sound using an array of rods that scatter the sound in all directions. In fact scientists in Hong Kong have created 'sonic' crystals from lead balls glued together with epoxy resin. Sonic crystals absorb sound and could be used to block sonar signals at sea so that submarines would be 'invisible'.

<< The network of holes block the seismic wave by scattering it in all directions >>

Test that theory

To test their 'crazy' idea about seismic waves the Spanish team drilled holes in a triangular and a honeycombed pattern in the marble floor of a local quarry. Each hole was 6 cm across, 160 cm deep and 14 cm from its neighbours. They dropped steel ball bearings on the ground to create vibrations. These vibrations would normally travel through the marble so that sensors could detect them – rather like the surface waves in an earthquake. The scientists placed their sensors, to detect how well the vibrations travelled through the lattice of holes. Both sets of holes damped down the vibrations considerably.

Impossible dream

Unfortunately, their calculations show that, if they want to use this for real seismic shielding, the holes would have to be hundreds of metres across and at least a kilometre deep. They could perhaps protect one building but to protect a whole town is obviously not feasible, yet. But, as one of the team comments, 'If we can use seismic shielding to reduce the earthquake by two points on the Richter Scale (or reduce its energy by 100 times) it would be great.'

Earthquakes start from a sudden movement of the Earth's crust where two continental plates are in contact. Immediately P-waves and S-waves travel through the Earth.

P-waves are longitudinal waves (the vibrations in the Earth are parallel to the direction the wave is travelling – like in a slinky) and travel fastest through a solid. They arrive at earthquake monitoring stations around the world first – so they are called *primary waves*. S-waves are transverse waves (the vibrations in the Earth are like the ripples on water). They travel more slowly, so arrive at earthquake monitoring stations later – so they are called *secondary waves*. Seismologists use the time delay between the P-waves and S-waves to work out exactly how far the earthquake is from the monitoring stations.

Surface waves travel round the Earth through the crust. It is the surface waves that cause all the damage during earthquakes.

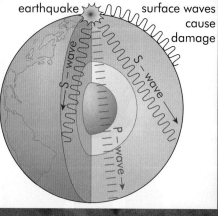

« The P-waves arrive at earthquake monitoring stations before the S-waves »

Protection from earthquakes

Earthquakes can be devastating and kill hundreds of people. Engineers are working on ways of building houses and offices that can withstand an earthquake. Unfortunately the 'earthquake proof' buildings in Mexico City suffered the worst damage when the 1985 earthquake hit! If the residents could be told to leave at the appropriate time, earthquakes would pose less of a risk. However not only is it impossible to predict when an earthquake will occur, it is impossible to say how severe it will be. There is an earthquake almost every day somewhere in the world but most are not even felt by people.

Predicting the unpredictable

Earthquakes happen when two continental plates shift suddenly. Of course it's not easy to say when this will happen. The plates move slowly (at about the same speed your fingernails grow) but continuously and the stresses build up for years. There's no pre-set point when they will finally 'give'. Predicting earthquakes has never been an exact science. In fact it has never been a science, until now.

Preventing earthquakes

If earthquakes happen because of friction betwen the plates, some people have suggested injecting lubricating fluids into the faults so that the plates slide past each other more smoothly. Others suggest forcing the rocks apart by using high pressure steam to open up the cracks.

Learning from animals and water levels

Some people claim that dogs howl and chickens flee roost before a significant earthquake. Scientists

« People say that dogs howl before an earthquake – but how true is this? »

are studying animals to see if they sense something that might help to predict earthquakes.

Chinese seismologists claim to be able to predict earthquakes by watching the level of water in wells. They say that stress in the rocks squeezes the water upwards. The levels of the radioactive gas radon may also rise and some scientists think that changes in the ground's electrical resistance or magnetism may hold clues.

Watching from the skies

The most likely way of predicting earthquakes will probably come from satellite monitoring. Using lasers that bounce off reflectors on satellites, seismologists can make amazingly accurate measurements of the movement of the Earth's crust. By monitoring the slight shifts in the Earth's crust it may be possible, soon, to be able to say that an earthquake is on the way. Already there are 45 observatories in 30 countries using lasers and satellites. They are so accurate they can pick up movements of a fraction of a centimetre over thousands of kilometres.

Watching underground

There is also an International Data Centre in Vienna that receives seismic data from over 320 stations around the world. They can pick up vibrations and immediately locate everything from a major earthquake to an underground explosion. This has an added bonus that if a country is

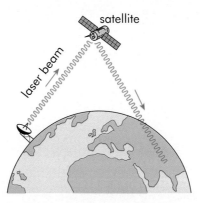

« Lasers and satellites can measure the tiniest movement in the Earth's crust »

testing nuclear weapons using underground explosions, its neighbours soon find out! On a particular day in May 1998, there were 58 seismic events detected. Fifty-seven were due to minor earthquakes, one was because India tested a nuclear weapon. Nothing is secret anymore! ■

Primary waves can travel faster through the inner core than through the outer core. This tells us the Earth's inner core is solid.

Secondary waves cannot travel through the outer core. This tells us the outer core is liquid.

Most of the Earth (the bit between the core and the crust) is solid **but** it can be squeezed by pressure like modelling clay or potty putty. The tectonic plates move around on this layer. Earthquakes happen along the cracks between these plates as the plates grind together.

Questions

1 **a)** How do the Spanish scientists plan to protect towns from earthquake damage?
   b) Why is this unlikely to be feasible?

2 What causes an earthquake?

3 Explain the difference between P-waves, S-waves and surface waves.

4 **a)** Why is it useful to be able to predict earthquakes?
   b) Why is it so difficult?

5 Using satellites seems to be the most promising method of predicting earthquakes. How does this work?

WEBSITES

www.earthquakes.bgs.ac.uk

www.scienceware.com

An e-mail from Hubble

Astronomer Malcolm Coe from the University of Southampton has just received his first extra-terrestrial e-mail. It came from his friend, John Grunsfeld who is an astronaut. John was flying in the Space Shuttle on his way to upgrade some apparatus on the Hubble Space Telescope. Malcolm can't tell us what was in the e-mail because it's classified 'confidential' but he can tell us a bit about his friend's work on the Space Shuttle.

« Malcolm Coe, astronomer from the University of Southampton »

« John Grunsfeld went up in the Space Shuttle to upgrade the Hubble Space Telescope »

Q. Was it a surprise to get an extra-terrestrial e-mail?

Malcolm: Yes, John had invited me to go to Florida in the USA to watch the launch of the Space Shuttle that he was flying on. It was an amazing experience. When I got back I sent him an e-mail and expected him to reply when the Space Shuttle returned ten days later. Instead I got a reply the next day!

Q. So what was your friend doing on the Space Shuttle?

Malcolm: The Hubble Space Telescope has a planned programme of upgrades over the 10–20 years of its lifetime. So, every so often the Space Shuttle goes up to fit new parts. This time John was fitting an upgraded camera to give a wider view of what the universe looks like. We want to be able to look at tens of thousands of galaxies and take pictures of a million stars at the same time. That's not possible with a tiny camera. Now, we can look forward to even more spectacular pictures from Hubble in the near future!

Q. Why is it important to get this wider view of the universe?

Malcolm: It's important to know why the universe looks like it does on a very large scale. How did it get to look like this? To do this we need to look at lots of galaxies and make sure we're not drawing conclusions from what we see in a quirky part of the universe. That would not be good science.

Q. What is Hubble looking for?

Malcolm: One thing Hubble has done is to look for other planets in our galaxy. We can tell there's a planet orbiting a star because we can see the star wobble a tiny amount as the planet goes round it and the force of gravity between the planet pulls on the star. Up to now we've seen 75 extra-solar planets in our galaxy. They're all relatively nearby – within 100 light years of us. That's 950 000 000 000 000 kilometres – too far to go for the weekend!

EDWIN HUBBLE

Edwin Hubble's father wanted him to be a lawyer but Edwin wanted to be an astronomer. It was a very fashionable and glamorous thing to do in the early 20th century when photography was being developed.

In the 1920s everyone thought that our Milky Way was the whole universe and that the other fuzzy clouds they could see (they called them nebulae) were on the outer edges of our Milky Way galaxy. Of course the photographs were not very good, so it wasn't easy to make

« Edwin Hubble – the first person to work out that the universe is expanding »

out exactly what these nebulae were. Hubble was the first person to work out that these clouds were actually separate galaxies and they weren't part of our Milky Way – they were much further away.

Hubble went further than that. He noticed that the light from these distant galaxies seemed to be the wrong wavelengths compared with what you get on Earth. It was redder than it should be. He called this the 'Red Shift'. He worked out that, just as a police siren sounds lower in pitch as it goes away from you, the red shifted light from the galaxies meant they were going away from us. And more than this! He worked out that the further away the galaxy, the faster it was moving!

This came as a complete surprise to everyone – except Einstein who was pleased to find that Hubble's expanding universe was exactly what his calculations had predicted. It was only one small step from there to ask how the universe started. If it was expanding it must have been smaller. And the smallest you can get is a point. The universe must have started expanding from one point. And this is how the idea of the 'big bang' first started.

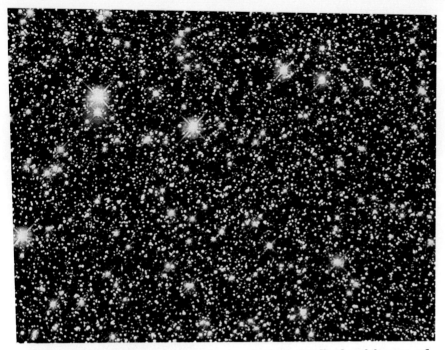

« Hubble is looking at stars in our galaxy to find evidence of planets – and even life! »

Q. And is there any chance of life on these other planets?

Malcolm: To work that out we need to know how intelligent life evolved on our planet. We think that how a solar system develops in the early stages is very important. For example during the first billion years (our Solar System is between five and seven billion years old now) our Solar System was not a very pleasant place to be – suffering under a very heavy meteor bombardment. The question is how did early life forms survive in this unpleasant environment? Perhaps it needed an injection of life from outer space to get it going! When we look at extra-solar planets we first have to check whether that solar system had the same conditions in its first billion years as ours did. If it didn't, then life may not have been

able to form and there's no point in looking further.

Q. Are there any planets that look likely to have life?

Malcolm: So far all the planets we have seen are in the wrong place. I think it will be another ten years before we find an earth-like planet. What's interesting is that all the extra-solar planets we have seen have been gas giants, like Jupiter and Saturn in our Solar System. In our Solar System we have rocky planets close to the Sun and gas giants further away. What's odd about all 75 of these extra-solar planets is that they seem to be too close to their suns. The question is, where are the rocky planets? We believe that life can only exist on rocky planets so that's what we are looking for. The other problem is that if gas giants can exist so close to their suns, a lot of

what we believe about how the Solar System formed is wrong. We may have to re-write all the textbooks!

Q. Does this mean our Solar System is odd?

Malcolm: It does seem to suggest that our Solar System is exceptional. But that is unlikely to be true. There have to be other solar systems like ours out there.

Q. Does the Hubble Space Telescope spend all its time looking for extra-terrestrial life?

Malcolm: No, Hubble is taking lots of readings all the time and astronomers all over the world are using the results and trying to learn more about the universe. We want to answer the really big questions like how it all started and how it will end, for example.

Q. Has Hubble come up with any answers to those questions yet?

Malcolm: One thing Hubble hasn't been able to answer is where is all the 'dark matter' and what is it made of. This is one of the big conundrums. We can see from the way galaxies behave that there is far more matter in them than we can see – about ten times as much! We can see stars, planets, asteroids, dust, and so on. If we work out the total mass of that lot we find the answer is far too small. There's all this matter spread throughout the galaxy that we just can't detect. That's what we call 'dark matter'. It has to be

there but so far we haven't found it.

Q. Is it important how much matter there is in the universe?

Malcolm: Well we all know that the universe started with the 'big bang'. The universe is expanding all the time and only gravity can eventually slow it all down. If there is enough matter in the universe, then the force of gravity will be strong enough to slow down the expansion and even start to make the universe contract. This means it will all end in a 'big crunch'. At the moment we don't think there is enough matter in the universe to cause a big crunch. We have a good idea how much matter there is. It's just intriguing that we can't seem to find a lot of it!

Q. Does anyone have any idea what this 'dark matter' is like?

Malcolm: There are lots of ideas. 'Dark matter' might be linked to other matter, so there might be 'dark matter' in this desk – or even several 'dark matter' desks' worth! Or 'dark matter' might be evenly spread through space. Britain is leading the way in the 'dark matter' search. There is a team of scientists in Yorkshire that has built apparatus to try to detect 'dark matter'. They have to work underground in a disused mine. This way their apparatus isn't affected by cosmic rays from outer space. They don't yet have any results, but it really is a fascinating topic. ▪

Questions

1 What is the evidence that the universe is expanding?

2 If the universe is expanding, what do scientists think started it off?

3 Do scientists think it will go on expanding forever? What could make it start to contract into a 'big crunch'?

4 The Hubble Space Telescope is looking for evidence of planets around other stars (among other things!).
   a) What evidence is there that a star has a planet?
   b) How many planets have they found so far?

5 Does it seem likely that these planets have intelligent life on them? Explain your answer.

6 What they have found so far may make the scientists re-write the textbooks. Why is this?

7 Malcolm talked about 'dark matter'.
   a) Why are scientists looking for 'dark matter'?
   b) What ideas do scientists have about 'dark matter' so far?

8 Malcolm obviously knows a lot about what the other scientists in his field are doing. How do you think he does this?

9 It is obvious that there are a lot of astronomers with different ideas about things like 'dark matter' or how life formed on early planets. How do you think they will resolve their differences?

Extra activities

Look at the NASA website at http://www.nasa.gov to find out about Hubble's search for planets. (You can enter 'Hubble' as a search word to give you more information.)

Hair today

There is a material that only exists as fibres about 0.05 mm diameter and up to about 1 m long. If you stretch it from 1 m to 1.25 m it will still spring back to its original length. And even though it is so fine you can hang weights of up to 10 N on it without it breaking. It is extremely flexible. What is it? It's your hair.

« There's a lot of science involved in keeping your hair beautiful »

Companies like L'Oreal use a whole range of physics techniques to help them understand the structure of human hair and to measure the effectiveness of shampoos, conditioners, colourants and perms.

The first thing that scientists need to know is the internal and external structure of the hair so that they can experiment on how different treatments affect the hair's properties. They use high-power X-rays that can be focused down to 0.001 mm diameter to probe the hair. As the X-rays go through the hair they are diffracted. A computer will analyse the diffraction pattern and work out the distances between individual cells and molecules and how they are arranged in each hair.

It turns out that your hair fibre is made of different types of dead cells filled with proteins called keratins. In the centre of the hair is the cortex. The cortex is made of long cells that line up along the length of the hair. Each long cell in the cortex is made of a bundle of macrofibrils embedded in a protein matrix or 'glue'. Inside each of these macrofibrils are smaller filaments (called intermediate filaments) and these smaller filaments are made of helix-shaped chains of molecules. The helix shapes are being formed about ten per second as your hair grows by about 15 cm a year.

Scientists at L'Oreal have used the X-ray diffraction pattern of hair that has been permed and compared it with normal hair. The pattern showed that the intermediate filaments in the cortex were closer

« High-tech X-ray diffraction can tell scientists which products really benefit your hair »

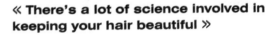

detector

X-rays

hair

together in permed hair than in untreated hair. They think this means that the matrix surrounding the filaments has been affected by the perm chemicals, but not the filaments themselves. This is why the hair is still strong even after perming.

They also found that the intermediate filaments were affected when the hair was over-processed (i.e. treated for too long or incorrectly). But this time the coiled helices at the centre of the filament became muddled and they were no longer perfectly

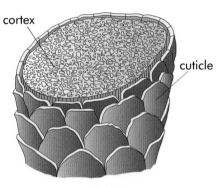

« The cuticle cells are held together by 'cement'. Scientists are trying to make products that repair the outer cuticle »

aligned along the length of the hair. This means the hair stretches too easily and breaks too easily. There is no treatment that can reverse this damage.

Around the outside of the hair cortex is the cuticle. This is made of a thick layer of flat overlapping cells. Its job is to protect the cortex in the centre of the hair. The cuticle cells are held together by intercellular cement which is made from proteins and natural oils and waxes (lipids).

One type of these lipids is the ceramides. These are essential to the cuticle. Scientists at L'Oreal have succeeded in making a molecule called 'Ceramide-R' which is similar to the natural ceramides in the hair. By attaching some radioactive carbon-14 to the Ceramide-R molecule it could be labelled and they watched where it attached itself on the hair. They then used the labelled Ceramide-R in shampoos and conditioners to treat normal hair. They found that the Ceramide-R filled the gaps in the intercellular cement where the hair was damaged.

Then they fired a beam of ions at the treated hair to blast away the cuticle and find out if the Ceramide-R had gone further into the hair. They found the Ceramide-R had migrated between the external scaly layers of the cuticle so that it helped the cuticle cells to stick together. This makes the hair stronger and less likely to stretch and break.

'So, they say, beauty is only skin deep'. Physics can probe deeper than that and give us answers to how to seem more beautiful. ■

Questions

1. If a human hair is 0.05 mm diameter and 1 m long, what is its volume?

2. Your hair is made of dead cells filled with proteins. What are these proteins called?

3. What is in the centre of a hair and what is it made of?

4. The smallest filaments in the centre of the hair are described as helix-shaped chains of molecules. What does 'helix-shaped' mean?

5. If your hair forms ten helix shapes per second as your hair grows, how many does it form in a year?

6. If your hair grows 15 cm per year, how much does it grow per second (in cm)?

7. How much hair have you had cut off since you were born?

8. What is on the outside of the hair?

9. The outer cells of hair are held together by lipids. What are lipids?

10. Why are scientists trying to make a molecule like the natural ceramides in the hair?

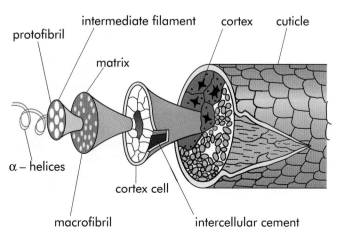

« Over-processing your hair causes it to weaken because the central filaments become muddled »

Are fuel cells the new batteries?

What's the link between the Space Shuttle and an ampoule of methanol that plugs into your personal stereo? They both use hydrogen to generate electricity. And fuel cells that use hydrogen to generate electricity could be the energy source of the future.

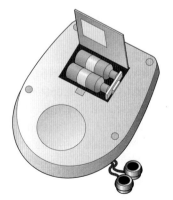

« Fuel cells in your personal stereo? Ampoules of methanol, instead of batteries that run down, could be the way things run in the future »

Fuel cells date back to 1836 when William Grove, a physicist, barrister and, later, a judge, demonstrated the first 'gas battery' at the Royal Institution in London, UK. They were an interesting novelty but of no practical use, so nothing happened for over 100 years.

But in the 1960s, NASA in the USA was looking for a suitable way to generate electricity for astronauts on the Apollo space missions. Batteries were too heavy and couldn't provide enough power. Hydrogen fuel cells, however, were ideal. They generated electricity as long as hydrogen was fed to them – and they had the rather useful bi-product of pure drinking water.

Now hydrogen is the fuel of choice for all Space Shuttle missions – and may well become the fuel that powers the 21st century.

Of course every hydrogen fuel cell needs hydrogen. Hydrogen is the most abundant element in the universe – it's just not found uncombined on Earth. It is,

however, found in many materials: natural gas, coal, methanol, biomass and water. There is, it seems, even the possibility of developing a type of algae that 'breathes out' hydrogen. The most perfect solution in most people's minds is extracting hydrogen from water by electrolysis – with the initial electric current produced either by solar cells or wind

« Hydrogen has been the fuel of space craft for years. Soon it may be what we all use every day »

turbines. We might even think of this as 'storing' renewable energy sources in the form of hydrogen and therefore overcoming the usual complaint that solar and wind power are seasonal and unreliable.

Fuel cells are very similar to batteries in the way they work. They both need ions moving from one electrode to another through an electrolyte, while the electrons flow through the circuit.

In a fuel cell hydrogen is fed to one electrode. Waiting at the other electrode is oxygen (from the air). Between the two electrodes is the electrolyte. This is a special polymer called Nafion. As with batteries, positive (hydrogen) ions flow through the electrolyte while the freed electrons travel round the external circuit. When the

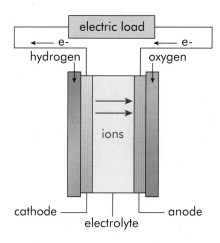

« **Hydrogen is fed to one side and oxygen to the other. The gases combine to make water and an electric current is produced. Perfectly clean fuel!** »

hydrogen ion appears at the second electrode, its picks up an electron and combines with the waiting oxygen to form pure water – the only waste product of the whole process.

Already almost every major car manufacturer in the world has a research and development

programme looking at fuel cells for powering cars. DaimlerChrysler has already announced it will be turning out 100 000 engines for its Mercedes A Class cars by 2005, while Ford's prototype fuel-cell car can accelerate from 0-60 mph in just over 14 seconds, compared with a diesel engined Mondeo, which takes a little under 14 seconds.

A 500 km journey will require 3 kg hydrogen. This may not seem much but at normal temperature and atmospheric pressure it takes 36 000 litres – the volume of several cars! This is less of a problem for buses – as can be seen by the fleet of buses in Vancouver and Chicago that run on hydrogen. But for the average motorist the idea of a giant hydrogen-filled balloon on the roof of the car is not attractive.

Some people are concerned that hydrogen is too flammable and that it may be dangerous. In fact it is no more flammable than petrol

Ions: Atoms with an outer electron removed, making them positively charged.

Electrons: Particles that orbit the atom – and also flow through conductors as an electric current.

Electrode: Metal plate which carries a positive or negative electric charge and attracts ions when immersed in a solution.

Electrolyte: Solution such as salt in water that will conduct electricity. The ions in the solution flow towards one of the electrodes.

« **All the major car manufacturers are working on fuel-cell cars. They seem a better bet than battery-driven cars** »

FORD FOCUS
FUEL CELL VEHICLE

size of a domestic fridge can power a house – both electricity and heating. There would be no more need for overhead power lines, or enormous power stations, and no danger of power cuts. The First Bank of Omaha has installed one already as even a brief interruption in their electricity supply causes it to lose millions of dollars in lost credit card transactions.

By 2050, we may have an energy supply system that produces no pollution, no acid rain, and no global warming. There will be no giant power stations or overhead power cables trailing across the countryside. And with no reliance on Middle Eastern oil, international trade balances will be very different. ∎

vapour and we are used to keeping that enclosed in tanks for safety.

One possible way to store the hydrogen is as a liquid at extremely low temperatures and high pressures – but the cost would be too high. Some scientists are working on special metal compounds called 'metal hydrides' that absorb hydrogen like a sponge – and hold it in a near liquid state until it is fed to the fuel cell. Others are working on carbon nanotubes (carbon in the form of tiny tubes) which also seem able to mop up hydrogen. The first hydrogen filling station – run cooperatively by Shell, Arco and Texaco – has already opened in the USA. It provides fuel for a fleet of cars run and serviced by DaimlerChrysler, Ford, Honda and Volkswagen.

In the meantime, it will be possible to run cars using fuel cells that run on methanol. These are more polluting and less efficient than hydrogen fuel cells – but much more environmentally friendly than petrol or diesel engines. The big

advantage is that methanol is a liquid so it can easily be pumped into a normal car fuel tank.

It's not just cars that will run on hydrogen. A fuel cell unit about the

Questions

1. Fuel cells are set to be the energy source of the future. But they have been around for a long time. Make a 'time-line' to show how fuel cells have been used over the years.

2. Fuel cells need hydrogen. What are the possible sources of hydrogen that the article mentions?

3. The article claims that fuel cells 'store renewable energy sources'. How can this be true?

4. Fuel cells are compared with batteries. How are they similar?

5. Draw a labelled diagram to show how a fuel cell generates electricity. Show the electrons travelling round the circuit while the ions travel through the electrolyte.

6. Why are car manufacturers interested in developing hydrogen fuel cell cars?

7. What problems are there with using hydrogen as a fuel in cars?

8. What answers does the article offer to these problems?

9. The article talks about other uses of hydrogen fuel cells. What examples does it give?

10. What benefits are there of moving to hydrogen as the main fuel for the 21st century?

C.V. Raman

– an invention before its time

There is a story that C.V. Raman, who was on a ship back to his home country of India, was contemplating the blue of the ocean, when he began to think about the way the light was reflecting off the water. For many years scientists had assumed that when light reflected off a surface, it was the same wavelength as when it hit the surface. It was certainly well known that any object appeared coloured because it reflected a certain colour from the spectrum and absorbed the rest. Then, to everyone's surprise in 1922 an Austrian physicist named Smekal predicted that it was possible for light to interact with a material and be reflected back at a very slightly different wavelength. This is what C. V. Raman was thinking about on his long journey home.

When he got back to Calcutta he set up an experiment with his colleague Krishnan. He sent a beam of sunlight through a filter to get a single pure colour of light – a single wavelength. He aimed the sunlight at a large container of liquid and simply looked at the reflected light through another

Raman was awarded the Nobel Prize in 1928 for his work

slightly different coloured filter. And what they showed was that some of the light was reflected at very slightly different wavelength from

the original beam of light. He quickly published his results – and not a moment too soon. In Moscow, Landsberg and Mandelstram had been working on exactly the same experiment and almost immediately reported the same results.

Raman was awarded the Nobel Prize in 1928 for his work but nothing much happened with his idea until the laser was invented in 1960. Nowadays it is easy to buy a complete 'Raman' kit with a laser to give you the single wavelength light and electronic detectors to detect the reflected light and measure its exact wavelength. Couple this with a standard computer and scientists now have a fast and efficient way to look at the Raman effect on almost anything.

Scientists have not been slow to see just how much you can do with these Raman kits. Everything from lipstick to the blue dye on denim jeans, priceless works of art to the famous 'ice man' found buried under a glacier in the Alps, the insulation around underground cables to the rocks on the surface of Mars, have been probed by

Blue jeans have been found in wardrobes since the 19th century

what scientists now call Raman spectroscopy. Even forensic scientists are making use of the technique to work out what substances have been used to contaminate Ecstasy tablets for example.

Because Raman spectroscopy is a young technique, scientists are still finding out exactly what it can do – and how to get it to work properly. Scientists in France decided to try it out on denim. Blue jeans have been found in wardrobes since the 19th century and the average American now owns 7.2 pairs. Denims are traditionally dyed with indigo. These scientists borrowed some denim clothes from the collection at the Musee de la Mode et du Costume de la Ville de Paris to see whether Raman spectroscopy could find out if they had been dyed with indigo. By measuring the exact wavelengths of the reflected light you get a 'fingerprint' of the material. Different dyes will give slightly different wavelengths of reflected light when analysed by the

computer. They found that the Levi-Strauss and Lee jeans were dyed with traditional indigo but it seemed that cheaper garments definitely used cheaper dyes.

The ice man never owned a pair of jeans. But the quality of the objects found buried with him gave historians a lot of useful information about how he lived – and died. More interestingly, he was the best-preserved mummified body ever found – even though he is 2000 years older than the Pharaoh Tutankhamen. By using Raman spectroscopy on the ice man's skin and also on freeze-dried modern skin, scientists could tell the historians a lot about how he died and how he was so well preserved. It seems he froze to death before his remains were dried out by the ice – a bit like the process of freeze-drying used to preserve food today.

Collectors of priceless works of art need to be sure they have not just bought a fake and they need to make sure it is conserved properly so that it will last for generations and not fall apart or decay. Raman spectroscopy is now a standard process in museums around the world. By looking at the different paints that an artist used, the

scientists can detect modern paints that have been used to restore the original painting, or even work out that it is not an original! The glazes on ancient pottery can be a clue about where and when it was made. And conservators need to know what the dyes are that they have on ancient textiles, so that they can use the best solvents for cleaning and conserving the artefact – without dissolving the fragile material.

It's not just museums and archaeologist who use Raman spectroscopy. It's an ideal technique for identifying the ink used on a forged cheque and can even be used to identify the dye on a fibre from a carpet – and work out where the murder victim fell as he was killed. By working closely with car

Raman could never have foreseen where his ideas would lead

manufacturers, forensic scientists can now use a speck of paint left after a hit-and-run accident and work out the make and year of manufacture of the car.

As Raman sailed back to India he could never have foreseen where his ideas would lead. It is almost certain he never saw it helping to solve crimes or helping historians solve the riddles of past civilisations. ∎

Questions

1 Why is Raman's discovery so surprising?

2 Why was it important that he published his experiment quickly?

3 Why did it take a long time for anyone to find a real use for the Raman effect?

4 Make a list of all the uses for the Raman effect mentioned in the article.

5 Why are art collectors interested in Raman spectroscopy?

ACKNOWLEDGEMENTS

I would like to acknowledge the following for the help and information given: *How cool can you get?* – Physics department, Royal Holloway, University of London; *Is there a future for scientists in space?* – Physics World Magazine; *The Sky is Falling* – Surrey space Technology Ltd, University of Surrey, Guildford; *Kirn Akran – certified moon rock handler* – University of Reading; *Jessica Cheung* – University of Reading; *ISIS – the biggest in the world!* – scientists at RAL; *A day in the life…* – Physics department, Royal Holloway, University of London; *An email from Hubble* – Malcolm Coe at Southampton University; *X-rays – promises and threats* – Paul Sellin, University of Surrey; *Time Travel* – Jim Al-Khalili, University of Surrey.

Bell Telephone Laboratories, **6** (courtesy of AIP Emilio Segre Visual Archives); Science Photo Library **8** (Charlotte Raymond); University of Lancaster **9**; Science Photo Library **10**; Science Photo Library **11r** (Space Telescope Science Institute/NASA); Science Photo Library **12l** (Hank Morgan); Corbis **12b** (W. Perry Conway); Corbis **13** (John Conrad); Science Photo Library **14** (Library of Congress); Science Museum/Science & Society Picture Library **15l**; Corbis **15r** (Bettmann); Science Museum/Science & Society Picture Library **17**; Science Photo Library **19**; Science Photo Library **20t** (Robin Scagell); Journal of the Royal Astronomical Society **20m**; Science Photo Library **20b** (Nick Sinclair); Corbis **22**; NASA **23b, 24**; Science Photo Library **26** (Mike Agliolo); NASA **27**; Science Photo Library **29** (Beinat Jerrican); Mediscan **30**; NASA **32**; Take One Photography **33**; Roger J. Stewart, University of Reading **36, 37**; Science Museum/Science and Society Picture Library **38**; **39** Science Photo Library **41** (John Mead), **42t**; Science Photo Library **42m** (David Hay Jones); Science Photo Library **42b** (David Frazier); Science Photo Library **43t** (Astrid & Hanns-Frieder Michler); Science Photo Library **43b** (Gary Parker); Science Museum/Science & Society Picture Library **44b**; Science Photo Library **45t** (Mahau Kulyk); DHA/NMPFT/Science & Society picture Library **45b**; Department of Clinical Radiology, Salisbury District Hospital/Science Photo Library **53**; Paul Sellin, Surrey University **54t**; Rutherford Appleton Laboratories **57;** Science Museum/Science & Society Picture Library **58**; Rutherford Appleton Laboratories **60**; Royal Holloway **61, 63, 64**; Corbis **66** (Lynda Richardson); Corbis **68b** (Mark M. Lawrence Photography); Science Photo Library **69b**; Space Telescope Science Institute/NASA/Science Photo Library **70**; Science Photo Library **71** (Detlev Van Ravensway); Powerstock **72**; NASA/Science Photo Library **74**; Ford Motors **75, 76**.

Every effort has been made to trace all the copyright holders, but if any have been overlooked the publisher will be pleased to make the necessary arrangements at the first opportunity.

INDEX